A Guide to
Lean Six Sigma
Management Skills

A Guide to
Lean Six Sigma
Management Skills

Howard S. Gitlow

CRC Press
Taylor & Francis Group
Boca Raton London New York

CRC Press is an imprint of the
Taylor & Francis Group, an **Informa** business

Auerbach Publications
Taylor & Francis Group
6000 Broken Sound Parkway NW, Suite 300
Boca Raton, FL 33487-2742

© 2009 by Taylor & Francis Group, LLC
Auerbach is an imprint of Taylor & Francis Group, an Informa business

International Standard Book Number-13: 978-1-4200-8416-0 (Hardcover)

Library of Congress Cataloging-in-Publication Data

Gitlow, Howard S.
A guide to lean six sigma management skills / Howard S. Gitlow.
p. cm.
Includes bibliographical references and index.
ISBN 978-1-4200-8416-0 (alk. paper)
1. Six sigma (Quality control standard) 2. Total quality management. 3. Organizational effectiveness. 4. Job satisfaction. I. Title.

HD62.15.G536 2008
658.4'013--dc22

2008046614

Visit the Taylor & Francis Web site at
http://www.taylorandfrancis.com

and the Auerbach Web site at
http://www.auerbach-publications.com

Dedication

This book is dedicated to all the worker bees who want to enjoy their work and cut their uncompensated overtime, but have no idea of how to go about it. I hope they find out how in this book.

Contents

Preface

Many worker bees are highly respected and well paid, and you may believe that they are happy with their jobs. Do not be fooled by their smiles. Many of them dislike their jobs and are "burned out" at work. So, if you are a worker bee just trying to do your job, it is possible that you think your job is boring, draining, and depressing. And you have to do it for the rest of your work life!

Is there hope? Well, to answer that question, you need to answer two more questions. *First,* **do you think your boss can help you get out of your negative work experience?** *Second,* **can you do anything to rise above your negative work experience?**

Question 1: Can Your Boss Help You Get Out of Your Negative Work Experience?

The answer to the first question is a definite YES. Only your boss can change the structure of the system in which you work (your job). Most employees are powerless to modify policies and procedures, methods, rules, and schedules that create a negative work experience. So, what can bring about positive change in your work experience? One answer is that the top management of your company makes an executive decision to become a *Lean Six Sigma* organization. Are you scratching your head and wondering what a *Lean Six Sigma* organization is? And what does this mean to me? Well, becoming a Lean Six Sigma organization could be a life-altering event for you and your company. You will learn more about why this is the case as you read this book.

Question 2: Can You Do Anything to Rise Above Your Negative Work Experience?

Because you cannot change your work conditions, is there anything you can do to improve your work experience? The answer is YES because when executives start talking about Lean Six Sigma management (and they probably will), you can be *very* supportive to the idea. Now, executives, managers, and workers have a vehicle

(Lean Six Sigma management) through which they can work as partners toward a common goal. The goal is to create an exciting and energizing workplace to pursue the organization's mission statement. The first major objective of this book will be to answer Question 2.

The second major objective of this book is to present Lean Six Sigma management theories, tools, and methods from the worker bee's point of view. Addressing the second objective will largely resolve the first objective. Worker bees (employees) have as much desire (intrinsic motivation) to learn Lean Six Sigma as executives. Executives want to learn Lean Six Sigma to improve the bottom line of their organization, as well as to improve their professional skill set and effectiveness on the job. Worker bees want to learn Lean Six Sigma to be able to increase enjoyment in their work, to better understand the system in which they work, and finally, to reduce uncompensated overtime. The third major objective of this book is to explain how you can prevent daily crises from messing you up at work. This book aims to assist worker bees, and any executive who wants to know, in how to enjoy work.

Acknowledgments

I would like to acknowledge Stephen Alpert for his creative input for this book, and Shelly Gitlow for being my guiding light.

About the Author

Howard S. Gitlow, Ph.D., is the Executive Director of the Institute for the Study of Quality, Director of the Masters of Science degree in Management Science, and a professor of management science, School of Business Administration, University of Miami, Coral Gables, Florida. He was a visiting professor at the Stern School of Business at New York University (2007 and 2008), and a visiting professor at the Science University of Tokyo in 1990, where he studied with Dr. Noriaki Kano. He received his Ph.D. in statistics (1974), M.B.A. (1972), and B.S. in statistics (1969) from New York University. His areas of specialization are Lean Six Sigma Management, Dr. Deming's theory of management, Japanese Total Quality Control, and statistical quality control.

Dr. Gitlow is a Six Sigma Master Black Belt, a Fellow of the American Society for Quality, and a member of the American Statistical Association. He has consulted on quality, productivity, and related matters with many organizations, including several Fortune 500 companies.

Dr. Gitlow has authored or co-authored many books including *Design for Six Sigma for Green Belts and Champions*, Prentice-Hall (2006); *Six Sigma for Green Belts and Champions*, Prentice-Hall (2004); *Quality Management: Tools and Methods for Improvement*, 3rd edition, Richard. D. Irwin (2004); *Quality Management Systems*, CRC Press (2000); *Total Quality Management in Action*, Prentice-Hall (1994); *The Deming Guide to Quality and Competitive Position*, Prentice-Hall (1987); *Planning for Quality, Productivity, and Competitive Position*, Dow Jones-Irwin (1990); and *Stat City: Understanding Statistics Through Realistic Applications*, 2nd edition, Richard D. Irwin (1987). He has published over 55 academic articles in the areas of quality, statistics, management, and marketing. While at the University of Miami, Dr. Gitlow has received awards for outstanding teaching, writing, and published research articles.

Chapter 1

The Meaning and Purpose of Work

1.1 Traditional View of Work

1.1.1 Doing Your Job

Do you enjoy your work? If your answer is yes, great for you! But if your answer is no, then consider the following. Are you denied the freedom to use your talents, skills, and creativity on the job? Are your skills, knowledge, and talent being underused, or abused? Do you get the "Sunday night blues"? If your answers to the above questions are yes, you are burned out at work! Many people say, "Work is called work for a reason."

As amazing as it may seem, work does not have to be a drain on your energy. It can actually fill you with energy, if you enjoy what you do and look forward to doing it, day after day and year after year. Many artists, athletes, musicians, and professors enjoy their work over the course of their lives. You can enjoy your work also, or at least you can enjoy it much more than you currently do. It just requires a redefinition of work, and a management team that promotes the redefined view of work. This book will explain how it is possible for you to enjoy your work and cut your uncompensated overtime, *assuming that executives do not crush the effort!*

Additionally, worker bees can learn Lean Six Sigma to know what their bosses are doing wrong to protect their self esteem; so they realize that they are not the problem, that the boss's system is the problem. This is a big realization!

1.1.2 Reacting to Daily Crisis

Most people go into work every day and are confronted with a long list of crises that requires immediate attention. For example, Sarah is an administrative assistant in a department in a large, urban, private university. She comes to work every day to be greeted by a long "to-do" list of mini-crises that are boring and repetitive. The mini-crises include answering the same old questions for faculty and students, week after week after week. What room is my class in? Does the computer in Room 312 work? What are my professor's office hours? Do you have the copies I requested for class 5 minutes ago? Blah, blah, blah. These crises prevent Sarah from doing her "real" work, which keeps piling up. It is all very frustrating and depressing. If you ask people what their job is, they may say, "I do whatever has to be done to get through the day without a major blow-up. Yech."

So, how can you prevent daily crises from messing you up? The third major objective of this book is answering this question.

1.2 Lean Six Sigma View of Work

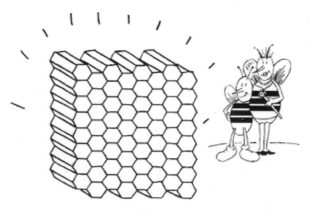

1.2.1 A New Perspective on Life and Work

Lean Six Sigma embraces nine principles which, when understood, may cause a transformation in how you view life in general, and work in particular. The nine principles are listed below.

Principle 1: Life and business are processes.
Principle 2: All processes exhibit variation.
Principle 3: Two causes of variation exist in many processes.
Principle 4: Life and business in stable and unstable processes are different.
Principle 5: Continuous improvement is economical, absent capital investment.
Principle 6: Many processes exhibit waste.
Principle 7: Effective communication requires operational definitions.
Principle 8: Expansion of knowledge requires theory.
Principle 9: Planning requires stability.

These principles are presented below and illustrated from the point of view of everyday life. Later in the book, they are illustrated from the perspective of work.

1.2.1.1 Principle 1: Life and Business Are Processes

A process is a collection of interacting components that transforms inputs into outputs toward a common aim, called a "mission statement." Processes exist in all facets of life in general, and organizations in particular, and an understanding of them is crucial.

The transformation accomplished by a process is illustrated in Figure 1.1. It involves the addition or creation of time, place, or form value. An output of a process has "time value" if it is available when needed by a user. For example, one has food when one is hungry, or equipment and tools available when one needs them. An output has "place value" if it is available where needed by a user. For example, gas is in one's tank (not in an oil field), or wood chips are in a paper mill. An output has "form value" if it is available in the form needed by a user. For example, bread is sliced so it can fit in a toaster, or paper has three holes so it can be placed in a binder.

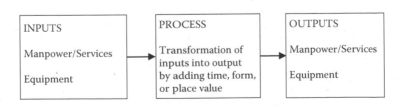

Figure 1.1   Basic process.

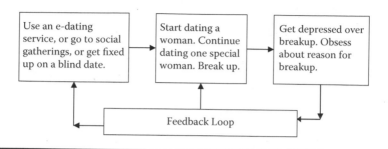

Figure 1.2 Ralph's relationship with women process.

An example of a personal process is Ralph's "relationship with women he dates" process. Ralph is 55 years old. He is healthy, financially stable, humorous, good looking, and pleasant. At age 45, he was not happy because he had never had a long-term relationship with a woman. He wanted to be married and have children. Ralph realized that he had been looking for a wife for 20 years, with a predictable pattern of 4- to 6-month relationships, that is, two relationships per year on average; see Figure 1.2. That meant he had about 40 relationships over the 20 years.

Ralph continued living the process shown in Figure 1.2 for more than 20 years. It depressed and frustrated him but he did not know what to do about it. Read the next principles to find out more about Ralph's situation.

1.2.1.2 Principle 2: All Processes Exhibit Variation

Variation exists between people, outputs, services, products, and processes. It is natural and should be expected but it must be reduced. The type of variation discussed here is the unit-to-unit variation in the outputs of a process (products or services) that cause problems down the production or service line, and for customers. It is *not* diversity — for example, racial, ethnic, or religious — to name a few sources of diversity. Diversity makes an organization stronger due to the multiple points of view it brings to the decision-making process.

Now go back to the discussion of unit-to-unit variation in the outputs of a process. The critical question to be addressed is: What can be learned from the unit-to-unit variation in the outputs of a process (products or services), to reduce it? Less variability in outputs creates a situation in which it is easier to plan, forecast, and budget resources. This makes everyone's life easier.

Example. Return to Ralph's love life. Ralph remembered the reasons for about 30 of his 40 breakups with women. He made a list with the reason for each one. Then he drew a line graph of the number of breakups by year (see Figure 1.3).

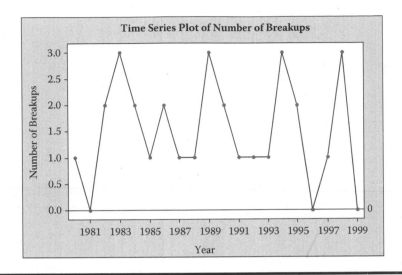

Figure 1.3   Time series plot of number of breakups, by year.

As one can see from Figure 1.3, the actual number of breakups varies from year to year. Ralph's ideal number of breakups per year is zero, assuming he is happy in a long-term relationship. The difference between the actual number of breakups and the ideal number of breakups is *unwanted variation*. Lean Six Sigma management helps one understand the causes of unwanted waste and variation, thereby giving one the insight needed to bring the actual output of a process and the ideal output of a process closer to each other.

Another example. Your weight varies from day to day. Your "ideal" daily weight would be some medically determined optimum level; see the black dots on Figure 1.4. One's "actual" daily weights may be something entirely different. One may have an unacceptably high average weight, with great fluctuation around the average; see the fluctuating squares on Figure 1.4. Unwanted variation is the difference between your ideal weight and your actual weights. "Lean Six Sigma" management helps one understand the causes of this variation, thereby giving one the insight needed to bring your actual weights closer to your ideal weight.

1.2.1.3 Principle 3: Two Causes of Variation Exist in Many Processes

There are two causes of variation in a process: (1) special causes and (2) common causes. Special causes of variation are due to assignable causes that are external to the process. Frequently, they are due to a particular person or some local situation.

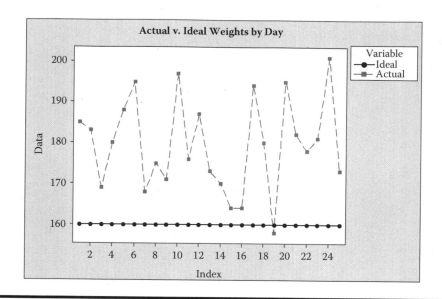

Figure 1.4   Actual versus ideal weights by day.

Common causes of variation are due to the process itself, that is, variation caused by the structure of the process. Examples of common causes of variation could be stress, values and beliefs, or the level of communication between the members of a family. Usually, most of the variation in a process is due to common causes [see Gitlow, Levine, and Popovich (2006); Gitlow and Levine (2004); Gitlow, Oppenheim, Oppenheim, and Levine (2004)]. A process that exhibits special and common causes of variation is unstable; its output is not predictable in the future. A process that exhibits only common causes of variation is stable (although possibly unacceptable); its output is predictable in the near future.

Dr. Walter Shewhart invented control charts in 1929 while working at the Bell Laboratories of the Western Electric Company. The top management of Bell Laboratories was confused as to why there was such a large amount of variation in the quality of telephones produced, given that there were such rigid specifications for incoming material and a tremendous amount of training on production methods for workers.

Shewhart developed a clever exercise to explain to management the difference between common and special causes of variation. He asked managers to write the lowercase letter "a" over and over again on a sheet of paper. At a haphazard point in each manager's writing of the "a"s, Shewhart would push his or her arm. The arm pushing caused that particular "a" to have a long tail. Figure 1.5 shows the results of one manager's experience.

aaaaaaaaaaaaaaaaaa------

Figure 1.5 One manager's experience with Shewhart's experiment to demonstrate common and special causes of variation in a process.

As one can see, the last "a" has a long tail. This is because Shewhart pushed the manager's arm while he was writing the last "a." The shape of the last "a" is affected by a special cause of variation, that is, Shewhart pushing the manager's arm. The differences in the sizes of all the other "a"s is due to common variation. The largest "a" is perhaps three times as big as the smallest "a." The variation in all the other "a"s is common variation that is due to the manager's ability to produce "a"s of consistent size. If one wants a particular manager to produce "a"s of more consistent size, then one could send that manager to a calligraphy class. Calligraphy training is an example of a possible process improvement designed to reduce common variation in the production of "a"s.

Example. Let us visit Ralph again. Ralph learned about common and special causes of variation and began to use some basic statistical thinking and tools to determine if his pattern of breakups with women was a predictable system of common causes of variation. Ralph constructed a control chart (see Figure 1.6) of the number of breakups with women by year. After thinking about himself from a statistical point of view using a control chart, he realized that his relationships with women were not unique events (special causes); rather, they were a common cause process (that is, his relationship with women process).

Control charts are statistical tools used to distinguish special from common causes of variation. All control charts have a common structure. As Figure 1.6 shows, they have a centerline, representing the process average, and upper and lower control limits that provide information on the process variation. Control charts are usually constructed by drawing samples from a process, and taking measurements of a process characteristic, usually over time. Each set of measurements is called a "subgroup" (for example, a day or month). In general, the centerline of a control chart is taken as the estimated mean of the process; the upper control limit (UCL) is a statistical signal that indicates any points above it are likely due to special causes of variation, and the lower control limit (LCL) is a statistical signal that indicates any points below it are likely due to special causes of variation. There are additional signals of special causes of variation that are not discussed in this book; see Gitlow, Levine, and Popovich (2006); Gitlow and Levine (2004); and Gitlow, Oppenheim, Oppenheim, and Levine (2004). Several

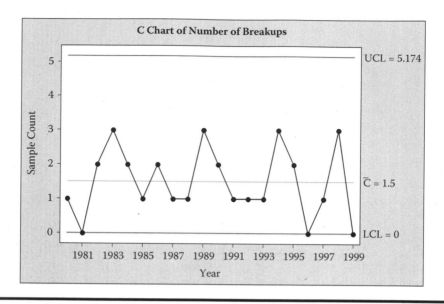

Figure 1.6 **Control chart of number of breakups with women, by year.**

software packages are available that do a nice job of creating control charts (for example, Minitab 15, www.minitab.com).

Back to Ralph's love life; Figure 1.6 shows that the number of breakups by year are all between the UCL = 5.174 and the LCL = 0.0. So, Ralph's breakup process with women only exhibits common causes of variation; it is a stable and predictable process, at least into the near future. This tells Ralph that he should analyze all 30 data points for all 20 years as being part of his "relationship with women" process; he should not view any year or any relationship as special.

Ralph was surprised to see that the reasons for the 30 relationships collapsed down to five basic categories, with one category containing 24 (80 percent) of the relationships. The categories (including repetitions) were grouped into the frequency distribution shown in Table 1.1.

A Pareto diagram is a type of bar chart that shows the biggest bar on the left side of the chart and the size of the bars decrease in size order as the chart moves to the right side; see Figure 1.7. A Pareto diagram can help one determine which of the categories on the x-axis are the "vital few" (big bars) common cause categories and which are the "trivial many" (small bars) common cause categories. This helps to prioritize efforts on categories with the largest bars, and hence the largest problems. A Pareto diagram of the data in Table 1.1 is shown in Figure 1.7.

Ralph realized that there were not 30 unique reasons (special causes) that moved him to break up with women. He saw that there were only five basic reasons (common causes of variation in his process) that contributed to his breaking up with women, and that "failure to commit" is by far the most repetitive common cause category.

Table 1.1   Frequency Distribution of Reasons for Breakups with Women for 20 Years

Reason	Frequency	Percentage
Failure to commit	24	80.00
Physical	03	10.00
Sexual	01	3.33
Common interests	01	3.33
Other relationships	01	3.33
Total	**30**	**100.00**

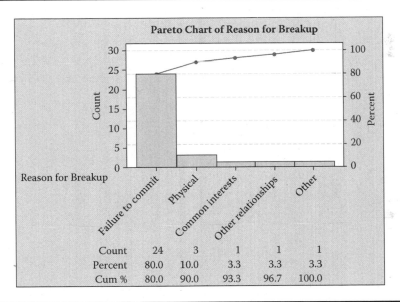

Figure 1.7   Ralph's Pareto diagram of reason for breaking up with women.

1.2.1.4 Principle 4: Life and Business in Stable and Unstable Processes Are Different

Principle 4 states that life and business in stable and unstable processes are different. This is a big principle. If a process is stable, understanding this principle will allow you to realize that all of the crises that bombard you on a daily basis are nothing more than the random noise (common causes of variation) in your life. Reacting to a crisis like it is a special cause of variation (when it is in fact a common cause of variation) will double or explode the variability of the process that generated it. All common causes of variation (formerly viewed as crises) should be categorized to identify "80-20 rule" categories that can be eliminated from the process. Eliminating an "80-20 rule" category will eliminate all, or most, future repetition of the common causes (repetitive crises) of variation generated by the problematic component of the process.

Example. Let us return to the example of Ralph. Ralph realized that the 30 women were not individually to blame (special causes) for the unsuccessful relationships, but rather that he was to blame because he had not tended to his emotional well-being (common causes in his "stable" emotional process); see Figure 1.6. Ralph realized he was the process owner of his emotional process. Armed with this insight, he entered therapy and worked on resolving the biggest common cause category ("80-20 rule" category) for his breaking up with women: "failure to commit"; see the biggest bar in Figure 1.7.

The root cause issue for this category was that Ralph was not getting his needs met by the women. This translated into the realization that his expectations were too high because he had a needy personality. In therapy he resolved the issues in his life that caused him to be needy, and thereby made a fundamental change to himself (common causes in his emotional process). He is now a happily married man with two lovely children. Ralph studied and resolved the common causes of variation between his ideal and real self, and moved himself to his ideal; see the right-hand side of Figure 1.8. He did this by recognizing that he was the process owner of his emotional process, and that his emotional process was stable and required a common cause type fix, not a special cause type fix. Ralph is the manager of his life; only he can change how he interacts with the women with which he forms relationships.

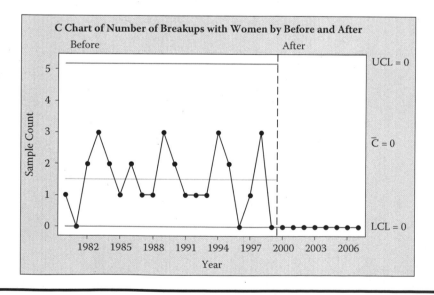

Figure 1.8 Control chart of number of breakups with women before and after therapy.

1.2.1.5 Principle 5: Continuous Improvement Is Economical, Absent Capital Investment

Continuous improvement is possible through the rigorous and relentless reduction of common causes of variation around a desired level of performance, in a stable process. It is economical to reduce variation around a desired level of performance, *without capital investment*, even when a process is operating within specification limits. For example, elementary school policy states that students are to be dropped off at 7:30 a.m. If a child arrives before 7:25 a.m., the teacher is not present and it is dangerous because it is an unsupervised environment. If a child arrives between 7:25 a.m. and 7:35 a.m., the child is on time. If a child arrives after 7:35 a.m., the entire class is disrupted. Consequently, parents think that if their child arrives anytime between 7:25 a.m. and 7:35 a.m., it is acceptable (within specification limits). However, Principle 5 promotes the belief that for every minute a child is earlier or later than 7:30 a.m., even between 7:25 a.m. and 7:35 a.m., a loss is incurred by the class. The further from 7:30 a.m. a child arrives at school, the greater the loss. Note that the loss may not be symmetric around 7:30 a.m. Under this view, it is each parent's job to continuously reduce the variation in their child's arrival time at school. This will minimize the total loss to all stakeholders of a child's classroom experience (the child, classmates, teacher, etc.). Table 1.2 shows the loss incurred by the class of children with respect to accidents from early arrivals of children and the disruptions by late arrivals of children for a one-year period.

Table 1.2 Loss from Minutes Early or Late

Arrival Times (a.m.)	No. of Minutes Early or Late	Loss to the Classroom
7:26	4	2 accidents
7:27	3	2 accidents
7:28	2	1 accident
7:29	1	1 accident
7:30	0	0 accidents
7:31	1	1 minor disruption
7:32	2	1 minor disruption
7:33	3	1 medium disruption
7:34	4	1 major disruption
Total		**6 accidents** **2 minor disruptions** **1 medium disruption** **1 major disruption**

Table 1.3 Improved Loss from Minutes Early or Late

Arrival Times (a.m.)	No. of Minutes Early or Late	Loss to the Classroom
7:26	4	0 accidents
7:27	3	2 accidents
7:28	2	1 accident
7:29	1	1 accident
7:30	0	0 accidents
7:31	1	1 minor disruption
7:32	2	1 minor disruption
7:33	3	1 medium disruption
7:34	4	0 disruptions
Total		**4 accidents** **2 minor disruptions** **1 medium disruption**

If parents can reduce the variation in their arrival time processes from the distribution in Table 1.2 to the distribution in Table 1.3, they can reduce the loss from early or late arrival at school. Reduction in the arrival time process requires a fundamental change in the parent's arrival time behavior, for example, laying out their child's clothes the night before to eliminate time. As one can see, Table 1.2 shows six accidents, two minor disruptions, one medium disruption, and one major disruption, while Table 1.3 shows four accidents, two minor disruptions, and one medium disruption. This clearly demonstrates the benefit of continuous reduction of variation, even if all units conform to specifications.

1.2.1.6 Principle 6: Many Processes Exhibit Waste

Processes contain both value-added activities and non-value-added activities. Non-value-added activities in a process include any wasteful step that (1) customers are not willing to pay for; (2) do not change the product or service; (3) contain errors, defects, or omissions; (4) require preparation or setup; (5) involve control or inspection; (6) involve over-production, special processing, and inventory; or (7) involve waiting and delays. Value-added activities include steps that customers are willing to pay for because they positively change the product or service in the view of the customer. Lean Six Sigma management promotes reducing waste through the elimination of non-value-added activities (streamlining operations), eliminating work in process and inventory, and increasing productive flexibility and the speed of employees and equipment.

Example. Recall Ralph and his "love life" dilemma. Well, if you consider Ralph's "failure to commit" as part of his "relationship with women" process, you can clearly see that it is a non-value-added activity. This non-value-added activity involves some wasteful elements. First, the women Ralph dates do not want to spend their valuable time dating a man who cannot commit to a long-term relationship. Second, the women ultimately feel tricked or lied to because Ralph failed to discuss his commitment issues early on in the relationship. Third, the women resent the emotional baggage (unwanted inventory) that Ralph brings to the prospective relationship. Clearly, Ralph needs to eliminate the above forms of waste from his "relationship with women" process.

1.2.1.7 Principle 7: Effective Communication Requires Operational Definitions

An operational definition promotes effective communication between people by putting communicable meaning into a word or term. Problems can arise from the lack of an operational definition such as endless bickering and ill will. A definition is operational if all relevant users of the definition agree on the definition. It is useful to illustrate the confusion that can be caused by the absence of operational definitions. The label on a shirt reads "75% cotton." What does this mean? Three quarters cotton, on average, over this shirt, or three quarters cotton over a month's production? What is three quarters cotton? Three quarters by weight? Three quarters at what humidity? Three quarters by what method of chemical analysis? How many analyses? Does 75 percent cotton mean that there must be some cotton in any random cross-section the size of a silver dollar? If so, how many cuts should be tested? How do you select them? What criterion must the average satisfy? And how much variation between cuts is permissible? Obviously, the meaning of 75% cotton must be stated in operational terms; otherwise, confusion results (see Deming, 1986, pp. 287–289).

An operational definition consists of (1) a criterion to apply to an object or to a group, (2) a test of the object or group with respect to the criterion; and (3) a decision as to whether the object or group did or did not meet the criterion (see Deming, 1986, p. 277). The three components of an operational definition are best understood through an example.

Mary lends Susan her coat for a vacation. Mary requests that Susan returns it clean. Susan returns it dirty. Is there a problem? Yes! What is it? Mary and Susan failed to operationally define "clean." They have different definitions of "clean." Failing to operationally define terms can lead to problems. A possible operational definition of "clean" is that Susan will get the coat dry-cleaned before returning it to Mary. This is an acceptable definition if both parties agree. This operational definition is shown below:

Criteria: The coat is dry-cleaned and returned to Mary.
Test: Mary determines if the coat was dry-cleaned.
Decision: If the coat was dry-cleaned, Mary accepts the coat. If the coat was not dry-cleaned, Mary does not accept the coat.

From past experience, Mary knows that coats get stained on vacation and that dry-cleaning may not be able to remove a stain. Consequently, the above operational definition is not acceptable to Mary. Susan thinks dry-cleaning is sufficient to clean a coat and feels the above operational definition is acceptable. Because Mary and Susan cannot agree on the meaning of "clean," Mary should not lend Susan the coat.

An operational definition of "clean" that is acceptable to Mary is shown below:

Criteria: The coat is returned. The dry-cleaned coat is clean to Mary's satisfaction or Susan must replace the coat, no questions asked.
Test: Mary examines the dry-cleaned coat.
Decision: Mary states that the coat is clean and accepts the coat. Or, Mary states the coat is not clean and Susan must replace the coat, no questions asked.

Susan does not find this definition of "clean" acceptable. The moral is: do not do business with people without operationally defining critical quality characteristics.

Operational definitions are not trivial. Statistical methods become useless tools in the absence of operational definitions because data does not mean the same thing to all of its users.

1.2.1.8 Principle 8: Expansion of Knowledge Requires Theory

Knowledge is expanded through revision and extension of theory based on systematic comparisons of predictions with observations. If predictions and observations agree, the theory gains credibility. If predictions and observations disagree, the variations (special and common) between the two are studied, and the theory is modified or abandoned. Expansion of knowledge (learning) continues forever.

Let us visit Ralph again. He had a theory that each breakup had its own and unique special cause. He thought deeply about each breakup and made changes to his behavior based on his conclusions. Over time, Ralph saw no improvement in his relationships with women; that is, the difference between the actual number of breakups by year was not getting any closer to zero, assuming a long-term relationship. Coincidentally, he studied Lean Six Sigma management and learned that there are two types of variation in a process: (1) special causes and (2) common causes. He used a control chart to study the number of breakups with women by year; see the left-hand side of Figure 1.8. Ralph developed a new theory for "his relationship with women" process based on his Lean Six Sigma studies. The new theory recognized that all of Ralph's breakups were due to common causes of variation. He categorized them, went into therapy to deal with the biggest common cause problem, and subsequently, the actual number of breakups with women by year equaled the ideal number of breakups with women by year; see the right-hand side of Figure 1.8. Ralph tested his new theory by comparing actual and ideal numbers, and found his new theory to be very helpful in improving "his relationship with women" process.

1.2.1.9 *Principle 9: Planning Requires Stability*

Plans are built on assumptions. Assumptions are predictions concerning the future performance of the processes required by the plan (see Deming, 1994, p. 103). Predictions have a higher likelihood of being realized if the processes required to deliver the assumptions are stable with low degrees of variation. That is, if you can stabilize and reduce the variation in the processes involved with the plan, you can affect the assumptions required for the plan. Hence, you can increase the likelihood of a successful plan.

Example: Jan was going to turn 40 years old. Her husband wanted to make her birthday special. He recalled that when Jan was a little girl, she dreamed of being a princess. So, he looked for a castle that resembled the castle in her childhood dreams. After much searching, he found a castle in the middle of France that met all the required specifications. It had a moat, parapets, and six bedrooms — perfect. Next, he invited Jan's closest friends, three couples and two single friends, filling all six bedrooms. After much discussion with the people involved, he settled on a particular three-day period in July, and signed a contract with the count and countess who owned the castle. Finally, he had a plan and he was happy.

As the date for the party drew near, he realized that his plan was based on two assumptions. The first assumption was that the castle would be available. This was not a problem because he had a contract. The second assumption was that all the guests would be able to go to the party. Essentially, each guest's life is a process. The question is: Is each "guest process" stable with a low enough degree of variation to be able to predict attendance at the party. This turned out to be a substantial problem. Due to various situations, several guests were not able to attend the party. One couple began to have severe marital problems. One member of another couple lost his job. Jan's husband should have realized that the likelihood of his second assumption being realized was problematic, and subject to chance; that is, he would be lucky if all the guests were okay at the time of the party. He found out too late that the second assumption was not met at the time of the party. If he had realized this, he could have saved money and heartache by renting rooms that could be cancelled in a small castle-type hotel.

1.2.1.10 Conclusion

This section presented nine principles that provide a different vantage point for viewing life. These principles can also be used to pursue "joy in work" and make it possible to say on Sunday night about tomorrow: "Thank God it's Monday!"

1.2.2 Doing Your Job and Improving Your Job

Most people go to work, day in and day out, struggle to meet their objective, quota, or work standard, and go home exhausted and depressed. This situation is reminiscent of the woodcutter who constantly complained about how he had to work so hard to meet his cut-tree quota, so he never had time to sharpen his axe. Basically, that is what happens if you just try to "do your job." But, there is great news. There is a better way. Instead of just doing your job, you can also improve your job, that is, sharpen your axe, or even invent a new tool or method for cutting your trees. Improving your job can actually make "doing your job easier and cut uncompensated overtime." Here is how it works.

You use the nine principles all at once, in concert with each other, to create a new view of work. The new view involves both doing your work and improving your work, then repeating both steps over and over again, always striving for perfection just like a pianist trying to perfect his or her playing.

1.2.2.1 Principle 1

Recall Principle 1: life and business are processes. So, you must view your job as a process, not as a series of unconnected crises. Many people mistakenly think only of production processes. However, administration, sales, service, human resources, training, maintenance, paper flows, interdepartmental communication, and vendor relations are all processes. Importantly, relationships between people are processes. Generally, processes can be studied, documented, defined, improved, and innovated.

It is the job of management to optimize the entire organization (process) toward its aim. This may require the suboptimization of selected components (subprocesses) of the organization; for example, a particular department may have to give up resources to another department in the short run to maximize profit for the overall organization.

If you do not view your job as a process, then it will become a chaotic and endless series of crises that you must deal with *before* you get to do your actual work. As the list of crises gets longer, so does your uncompensated overtime hours. Most of your crises are nothing more than the repetitive poor performance of your work processes. If these processes worked better, they would mess up less frequently, and you would have fewer crises to deal with before you could do your real job. So, how do you go about viewing your job as a process? Well, the first thing is to see your job as a flowchart. The simplest flowchart is shown in Figure 1.9.

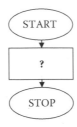

Figure 1.9 Simplest flowchart of work.

Figure 1.9 recognizes that your work is a process; it starts and stops each day but it acknowledges that you have not yet documented it; hence, the "?". So, the next step is to flesh out Figure 1.9 to a more detailed and useful representation of your job.

1.2.2.1.1 Aside on Flowcharts

A flowchart is a pictorial summary of the flows and decisions that comprise a process. It is used for defining and documenting the process. Figure 1.10 shows an example flowchart for a data entry operator in a call center. The day begins with punching in, turning on the computer, and getting settled. Next, the operator prioritizes his tasks for the day. Then the operator does the next task until it is complete. This occurs over and over all day until it is time for punching out.

A flowchart can help a manager, worker, or anyone else to understand, define, document, study, improve, or innovate a process.

The American National Standards Institute (ANSI) has approved a standard set of flowchart symbols that are used for defining and documenting a process. The shape of the symbol and the information written within the symbol provide information about that particular step or decision in a process. Figure 1.11 shows the basic symbols for flowcharting that standardize the definition and documentation of a process.

1.2.2.1.2 Advantages of a Flowchart

Flowcharting a process, as opposed to using written or verbal descriptions, has several advantages, to include:

- A flowchart functions as a communications tool because it is a pictorial view of the steps and decisions in a process that can be used by all stakeholders of the process.
- A flowchart shows the functions of personnel, workstations, and subprocesses in a system, and their interrelationships.
- A flowchart enables a viewer to spot logical errors and problems in a process.
- A flowchart documents a system.

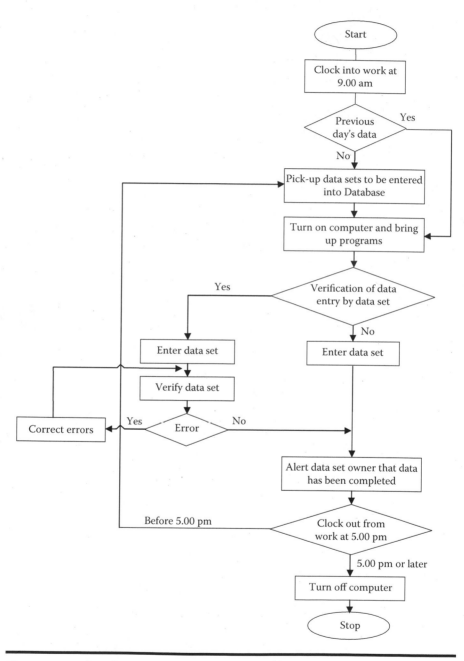

Figure 1.10 Flowchart of a data entry job.

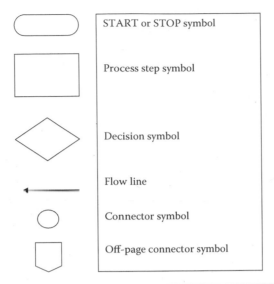

Figure 1.11   Flowchart symbols.

Flowcharts are simple to use, providing that appropriate following guidelines are followed, in keeping with standard practices. These guidelines are listed below.

- Flowcharts are drawn from the top of a page to the bottom and from left to right.
- Where the activity starts and where it ends should be determined.
- Each step of the activity should be described using "one-verb" descriptions (e.g., "prepare statement" or "punch-in to work").
- Each step of the activity should be kept in its proper sequence.
- The scope or range of the activity being flowcharted should be carefully observed. Any branches that leave the activity being charted should not be drawn on that flowchart.
- Use the standard flowcharting symbols as shown in Figure 1.11.

1.2.2.1.3 Constructive Opportunities to Change a Process

When using a flowchart, changing a process is facilitated by:

1. Finding the weak sections of the process (for example, sections with high defect rates)
2. Determining the parts of the process that are within the process owner's control
3. Isolating the elements in the process that affect customers

If these three conditions exist simultaneously, an excellent opportunity to improve a process has been found. In general, process improvements have a greater chance of success if they are either nonpolitical or have the appropriate political support, either do not require capital investment or have the necessary financial resources, and have the full commitment of the process owner.

Once you see your job as a process, or as a series of processes, you will realize that it is composed of small steps that may be changed or eliminated to make it better; for example, getting rid of unnecessary signatures on a form to reduce cycle time to process a monthly report.

In conclusion, an organization is a collection of subprocesses, all collectively building to the overall process that is the organization. All processes have customers and suppliers; these customers and suppliers can be internal or external to the organization. A customer can be an end user or the next operation downstream. The customer does not even have to be a human; it can be a machine. A supplier can be another firm providing subassemblies or services, or the prior operation upstream.

1.2.2.2 Principle 2

Recall Principle 2: all processes exhibit variation. Once you see your job as a process composed of small steps, you are ready to appreciate that the inputs and outputs for each step vary over time. They may vary so little that they are not detectable with state-of-the-art measuring devices; however, they still vary. No process is perfect; that is, all processes exhibit variation in their performance. The question is: Is the variation causing a problem? In many day-to-day situations, the answer is a definite yes. You probably suffer because of variation coming to you as input, or leaving you as output. You probably view this variation as a slew of crises that inundates you on a daily basis. For example, suppose you are a data entry operator. On each of 24 consecutive days, subgroups of 200 of your data entries are inspected by your supervisor. Table 1.4 shows the above data entry data.

Figure 1.12 is a plot of the fraction of defective entries as a function of time, that is, the number of data entries for a day divided by 200. It seems to indicate that on days 5, 6, 10, and 20, something unusually good happened (0 percent defectives); and on days 8 and 22, something unusually bad happened. You may find you get praised for days 5, 6, 10, and 20, and criticized for days 8 and 22. So, your second big lesson from the new perspective is that variation can cause ups and downs in the output of a process — that is, your work.

1.2.2.3 Principle 3

Recall Principle 3: two causes of variation exist in many processes — (1) common variation and (2) special variation. Common variation is inherent in every process. It is comprised of myriad sources that are always present in a process. Management should not hold workers responsible for such system problems; the

Table 1.4 Data Entry Data

Day	Entries Inspected	Defective Entries
1	200	6
2	200	6
3	200	6
4	200	5
5	200	0
6	200	0
7	200	6
8	200	14
9	200	4
10	200	0
11	200	1
12	200	8
13	200	2
14	200	4
15	200	7
16	200	1
17	200	3
18	200	1
19	200	4
20	200	0
21	200	4
22	200	15
23	200	4
24	200	1

system is management's responsibility. If management is unhappy with the amount of common variation in the system, it must act to reduce it. Special variation is created by causes that lie outside the system. Frequently, their detection, possible avoidance, and rectification are the responsibility of the people directly involved with the process. But sometimes management must try to find these special causes.

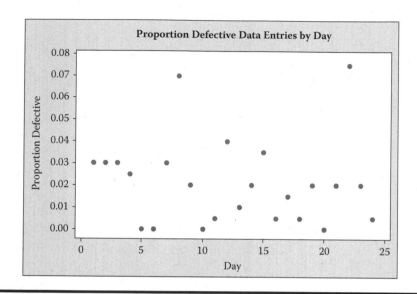

Figure 1.12 Plot of fraction of defective entries against time.

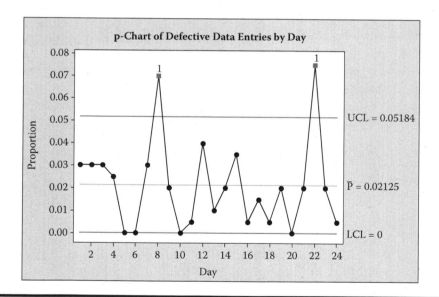

Figure 1.13 p-Chart of defectives.

When found, policy must be set so that if these special causes are undesirable, they will not recur. If, on the other hand, these special causes are desirable, policy must be set so that they do recur.

Once you realize that your job is a process that exhibits variation, then you can use "control charts" to distinguish between the two types of variation. Figure 1.13

shows the control chart (called a p-chart for proportion defective) for the data entry process from Table 1.4. It is likely that on days 8 and 22 there is some special variation. Note that the fractions defective on days 5, 6, 10, and 20 are not below the lower control limit (LCL). Days with no defectives are not out of control; we have merely observed that the process is capable of producing zero defectives 4 out of 24 days, or a sixth of the time. The observations on days 8 and 22 are above the upper control limit (UCL) and indicate that the process exhibits two special causes of variation.

When a worker determines that the cause of variation is special, he should search for and resolve the causes. This is best accomplished by keeping a log sheet (diary) of all the defective data generated by the process by day, as well as any unusual activity by day. Unusual activity could include a new worker or supervisor, new machinery, a new supplier, a process change, a change in corporate policy or procedure, to name a few examples. After the causes of special variation have been identified and rectified, a stable process will result, that is, a process that exhibits only common causes of variation.

In our example, to bring the process under control, a team of data entry operators investigates the observations that are out of control (days 8 and 22). In this case, they find from the log sheet that on day 8 a new operator was added to the workforce without any training. The logical conclusion is that the new environment probably caused the unusually high number of errors. To ensure that this special cause does not recur, management adds a one-day training program in which data entry operators are acclimated to the work environment.

The same team of data entry operators conducted an investigation of the circumstances occurring on day 22. Their examination of the log sheet reveals that on the previous night (day 21), one of the data entry terminals malfunctioned and was replaced with a standby unit. The standby unit is older and slightly different from the ones currently used in the department. Repairs on the regular terminal were not expected to be completed until the morning of day 23. To correct this special source of variation, the team recommends developing a proactive program of preventive maintenance on the terminals to decrease the likelihood of future breakdowns. Employees then implement the solution with the approval of management.

The process changes stemming from investigations of days 8 and 22 hopefully will stabilize the process. Consequently, the data from days 8 and 22 can now be deleted. After eliminating the data for the days in which the special causes of variation are found, the control chart statistics are recomputed. Figure 1.14 shows the revised control chart with days 8 and 22 eliminated. The process appears to be stable (in statistical control).

Figure 1.15 shows a Pareto diagram of all the remaining 73 data entry errors after dropping the data entry errors for day 8 (14 errors) and day 22 (15 errors). They are likely all due to common causes of variation. As you can see, "transposed and incorrect numbers" is the largest common cause category of repetitive problems.

A brainstorming session of the likely cause of "transposed and incorrect numbers" was poor lighting; so florescent lights were installed in the data entry department. A

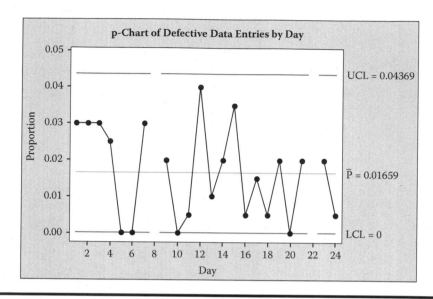

Figure 1.14 Revised control chart for proportion defective.

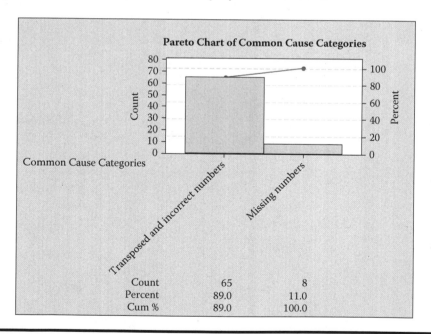

Figure 1.15 Pareto diagram of common causes.

control chart of the fraction of defective data entry errors before and after the installation of the florescent lights is shown in Figure 1.16. As you can see, the proportion of defective data entries is dramatically lower and stable with fluorescent lights.

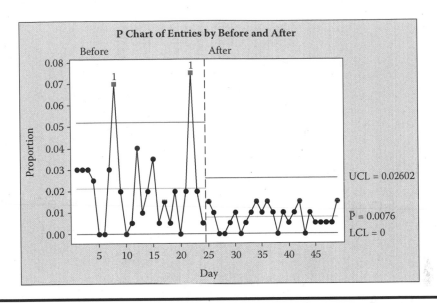

Figure 1.16 Control chart of proportion defective data entries before and after fluorescent lighting.

1.2.2.4 Principle 4

Recall that the rules for reducing variation in a stable process are entirely different from the rules for reducing variation in an unstable process. Generally, resolution of special causes of variation requires diagnosing the particular situation in which the variation occurred and setting policy to make the process robust in respect to its future impact; usually this is done by the person or people closest to the situation (workers or engineers on the line). However, reducing common causes of variation requires a study of the entire process (not just a particular situation) and a fundamental change to the process. Only the process owner (in an organization, this is management) can reduce common causes of variation by changing the flow, policies, and procedures of the process. Reduction of variation in a process requires an understanding of special and common causes of variation.

Consider the following example. Paul is a 40-year-old, mid-level manager who is unhappy because he wants his boss to give him a promotion. He thinks about his relationship with his boss and wonders what went wrong. He determines that over a period of 10 years he has had about 80 disagreements with his boss, two per quarter. Paul thinks about what caused each disagreement. Initially, he thought each disagreement had its own special reason. After listing and studying the pattern of the number of disagreements per year using a control chart, Paul discovered that it was a stable and predictable process of common causes of variation. Subsequently, he wrote down the reason for as many of the disagreements as he could remember (about 70); Paul keeps a diary. After thinking about his relationship with his boss from the perspective of common causes, he realized his disagreements with his boss were not unique events (special causes); rather, they were a repetitive process, and the reasons for the disagreements could be classified into common cause categories. He was surprised to see that the 70 reasons collapse down to four basic reasons (poor communication of a work issue, a process failure causing work not to be completed on schedule, unexcused absence, and pay-related issues), with one reason — poor communication of a work issue — accounting for 75 percent of all disagreements. Armed with this insight, he scheduled a discussion with his boss to find a solution to their communication problems. His boss explained that he hates the e-mails that Paul is always sending him and wishes he would just talk to him and say what is on his mind. They resolved their problem, their relationship greatly improved, and, eventually, Paul received his promotion.

If a process is not stable, two scenarios exist: (1) being able to distinguish special from common causes of variation, and (2) not being able to distinguish special from common causes of variation. In the first scenario, process owners can resolve special causes of variation by making process improvements to eliminate the effects of negative special causes of variation or to incorporate the effect of positive special causes of variation — for example, eliminating the negative effects of special cause data entry errors in an earlier example, then reducing common causes of variation for data entry errors by improved fluorescent lighting. The second scenario creates a sad reality. It is an existence in which people overreact to all variation regardless of whether it is special or common. This leads to increased variation in a process (see the funnel experiment to be discussed later), less predictability, and a marked deterioration in the "joy of work." Paul's initial situation mentioned above is an example of the second scenario.

1.2.2.5 Principle 5

Recall Principle 5: continuous improvement of a stable process is economical, absent capital investment. For example, the starting time for your job is 8:30 a.m. If you arrive before 8:25 a.m., you waste your time. If you arrive between 8:25 a.m. and 8:30 a.m., you get yourself situated and ready for the job. If you arrive between 8:30 a.m. and 8:35 a.m., you are okay. If you arrive after 8:35 a.m., the entire workplace is delayed until a replacement employee can be found. Consequently, you think arriving anytime between 8:25 a.m. and 8:35 a.m. is acceptable. However, Principle 5 promotes the belief that for every minute you are earlier or later than 8:30 a.m., even between 8:25 a.m. and 8:35 a.m., a loss is incurred either by yourself (early) or your fellow employees and management (late). The further from 8:30 a.m. you arrive to work, the greater the loss. Note that the loss may not be symmetric around 8:30 a.m. Under this view, it is your job to continuously reduce the variation in your arrival time to work. This will minimize the total loss to all stakeholders of your job (you, fellow workers, boss, suppliers, customers, etc.). A frequency distribution of the arrival times for the last 100 workdays is shown in Table 1.5.

Table 1.5   Arrival Time Distribution for 100 Days

Arrival Times (a.m.)	Frequency
8:26	01
8:27	06
8:28	11
8:29	19
8:30	25
8:31	20
8:32	08
8:33	08
8:34	02
Total	**100**

All the above data points conform to the acceptable arrival times of 8:25 a.m. to 8:35 a.m. Consequently, one would think all is well. However, under the notion of continuous improvement, there is a loss for every minute early or late. At an hourly pay rate of $60.00 per hour, the loss to the employee is $1.00 for every minute early. However, at an output rate of $60,000 per hour, the loss is $1,000.00 for every minute the employee is late. Under this view, the loss is not zero as it is under the view that all the arrival times are acceptable. Rather, the loss is $68,063; see Table 1.6. Please note that in this example, the entire delay time for the workplace is being placed on one employee; that is, everybody else is exactly on time.

If you can reduce the variation in your arrival time process from the distribution in Table 1.6 to the distribution in Table 1.7, you can reduce the loss from early or late arrival to work from $68,063 units to $50,050. Reduction in the arrival time process requires a fundamental change to your arrival time behavior, for example, laying out your clothes the night before to eliminate time wasted in clothes selection. This clearly demonstrates the benefit of continuous reduction of variation, even if all units conform to specifications.

1.2.2.6 Principle 6

Many processes contain waste. Recall from Principle 1 that a flowchart is a tool used to provide a "detailed picture" of a process. A "detailed picture" should provide the necessary specificity required to understand the process to be able to effectively eliminate waste from it. Team members eliminate waste through "lean thinking" to create a more efficient and effective process.

Table 1.6 Loss from Minutes Early or Late for 100 Days

Arrival Times (a.m.)	No. of Minutes Early or Late	Frequency	Loss ($)
8:26	4	01	04
8:27	3	06	18
8:28	2	11	22
8:29	1	19	19
8:30	0	25	00
8:31	1	20	20,000
8:32	2	08	16,000
8:33	3	08	24,000
8:34	4	02	8,000
Total		100	68,063

Table 1.7 Improved Loss from Minutes Early or Late

Arrival Times (a.m.)	No. of Minutes Early or Late	Frequency	Loss ($)
8:26	4	00	00
8:27	3	05	15
8:28	2	08	16
8:29	1	09	19
8:30	0	36	00
8:31	1	19	19,000
8:32	2	08	16,000
8:33	3	05	15,000
8:34	4	00	00
Total		100	50,050

In practice, "lean thinking" reduces the lead-time and the resources (waste) required between the delivery of a service or product and the start time of the process that requires the delivery.

Waste can exist in almost any area of an organization. The following list shows common areas in which waste is found in an organization:

- Supplier relations
- Plant or facility layout
- Procedures for setting up machines
- Procedures for maintaining equipment
- Training programs
- Measurement systems
- Work environment

Lean thinking (also called "lean management") promotes reduced complexity of processes, decreased cycle times, and lower costs through the elimination of waste (non-value-added steps in a process).

Team members can reduce waste through promoting *housekeeping* and reducing *complexity*. *Housekeeping* is a two-step process. The first step is the mundane but critical process of: (1) eliminating unnecessary "things" in the workplace so you can see the necessary "things" (for example, get rid of old files, broken copiers, etc.); (2) organizing necessary "things" in the workplace so they can be easily found (for example, place needed files, office suppliers, etc. in their proper place); (3) cleaning and maintaining the necessary "things" in the workplace (for example, wiping away dirt on computer screens, oiling motors, etc.); (4) making a habit of doing the above three activities the last five minutes of every day; and (5) spreading housekeeping throughout the organization. The second step is standardizing a process so that all the processes' stakeholders know what to expect from the process; that is, they all visualize the process as the same flowchart. *Complexity* is the creation of unnecessary steps in a process. It is frequently caused by overreactions to random noise in the workplace; that is, treating common causes of variation like special causes of variation. For example, if one employee brings a firearm to work in a 20-year period, requiring all employees to go through a metal detector might add unnecessary complexity to the "going to work" process.

1.2.2.6.1 Housekeeping: Step 1

The first step in housekeeping is frequently accomplished using the "5S" methods. The "5S" methods are very simple techniques for highlighting and eliminating waste, inconsistency, and unreasonableness from the workplace. Table 1.8 briefly describes each of the "5S"s, followed by detailed explanations.

1.2.2.6.1.1 Number 1: Seiri (Sort) — "Seiri" means to sort things using specific rules, and throw away unnecessary items, or at least remove them to a place where you can find them when needed. Putting away those things you are not going to use

Table 1.8 Description of the "5S"s

"S"	Rough Translation	Description
Seiri	Sort and throw away	Eliminate unnecessary things (or put them away) and make necessary things visible.
Seiton	Systematize (Orderliness)	Order essential things so that they can be quickly and easily accessed and put away.
Seiso	Spic & Span (Clean)	Clean machines, equipment, and the work environment.
Seiketsu	Standardize	Develop "best practices" to make the above "3S"s habits.
Shitsuke	Self-discipline	Get everyone to use the above "4S"s in work every day.

Table 1.9 Needs/Wants Analysis for All Items in a Workplace

Item	Needed Regularly			Needed Irregularly			Wanted (Needed Less Frequently than Yearly)	Not Wanted
	Needed Daily	Needed Weekly	Needed Monthly	Needed Quarterly	Needed Semi-annually	Needed Yearly		

today also means that the ones you are going to use today become more visible and easier to find. For Seiri to work, it is important for people to take personal responsibility for sorting and throwing away unnecessary "things" in their workplace.

Seiri requires that team members define the difference between *needed* items and *wanted* items; a needed item is an item that has been used within the past year, while a wanted item is an item that has not been used in the past year. Note that items necessary for legal requirements should be considered needed items.

Team members use Table 1.9 to sort each "thing" in the workplace as a wanted item or a needed item. It further subclassifies needed items into useful categories for actions to be discussed later in this book.

Table 1.10 Taxonomy for Red-Tagging "Needed Irregularly" Things

Categories	*Subcategories*	*Selected Examples of "Things" in Subcategories*
Offices	Documents	Memos, e-mails, reports, contracts, estimates, policies
	Equipment	Faxes, phones, computers, printers
	Supplies	Desks, chairs, shelves, file cabinets, storage boxes
	Stationery	Pens, pencils, scissors, tape
	Other	Reference books, forms, trade magazines
Work Areas	Inventory	Raw materials, Work in process, component parts, finished items
	Equipment	Machines, work desks and chairs, tools, jigs, bits
	Space	Operations areas, rest areas, walkways

One method for sorting "things" in a work area into the categories shown in Table 1.9 is called the "red-tag" strategy. First, team members red-tag and remove from the workplace all things that are obviously "not wanted." The unwanted items are then thrown away or sold. Removal of "not wanted" things makes it easier to see all remaining "wanted" and "needed" things. Second, team members red-tag all "wanted" and "needed irregularly" things using the classifications in Table 1.9. These red-tagged items are thrown away, sold, or put into remote storage.

A list of "needed irregularly" materials or items to be subjected to the red-tagging method is shown in Table 1.10. It is important to never red-tag people, not even as a joke.

Red-tagging promotes the principle of using "only what is needed, in the amounts needed, and only when needed." Table 1.11 provides a structure for red-tagging the "things" in a work area. Team members use Table 1.11 to determine the disposition of the things listed in Table 1.9.

Figure 1.17 is a photograph of a shelf unit in a work area that has experienced a red-tagging session.

Figure 1.18 shows before and after "red-tagging" photographs for three work areas in a plastic cup manufacturing process.

1.2.2.6.1.2 Number 2: Seiton (Systematize or Orderliness)

"Seiton" means tidily placing "things" in their proper places so anyone can access or put away the item. Individuals must follow five rules to put items away:

Table 1.11   Disposition Rules in a Work Area

Frequency of Use		Description	Organization Method
Not wanted things		(1) Defective materials and items (2) Things not wanted in your workplace or any other workplace in your organization	Discard or sell
Wanted (but not needed) things		Things used less than once per year	(1) Things are transferred to a workplace in your organization that needs them (2) Store in a remote location (3) Discard or sell (may require management approval)
Needed Things	Irregularly	Things used yearly	Store in a remote location
		Things used semi-annually	(1) Store in a remote location (2) Store near process where used
		Things used quarterly	(1) Store in a remote location (2) Store near process where used
	Regularly	Things used every month	Store near process where used
		Things used every week	Store near process where used
		Things used every day	Store in operation where used

1. Decide who should put things away.
2. Decide what things should be put away.
3. Decide where things should be put away.
4. Determine when things should be put away.
5. Determine how things should be put away (that is, the layout of things to be put away).

Never attempt to use Seiton (orderliness) without having first used Seiri (sorting). The above five rules are used to create orderliness for at least three categories of "things":

1. Spaces such as walls, shelves, floors, walkways, and storage areas
2. Materials and items such as raw materials, component parts, parts to be machined, in-process inventory, work in process, and finished products
3. Equipment such as machines, tools, jigs, dies, bits, gauges, carts, conveyance devices, tables, chairs, and cabinets

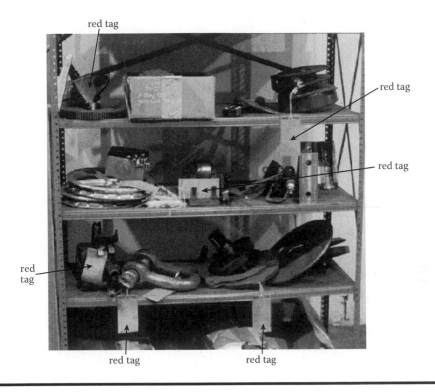

Figure 1.17   An example of red-tagging.

Orderliness can be promoted in all three of the above categories using:

■ Layouts of the workplace
■ Marks and signs
■ An inventory management system

Layouts of the workplace provide an overview for team members and employees to determine where "things" should be kept in the workplace. There are two types of layouts that can be used to promote orderliness: (1) overhead views and (2) frontal views. Overhead views give team members and employees a sense of what "things" can be stored in which locations (see Figure 1.19), as well as who sits in which locations (see Figure 1.20). The ultimate goal of overhead views is allowing a visitor to find an employee in the workplace without asking anyone for directions. This application is extremely valuable in workplaces that service customers. Note that overhead views should always have a colorful "You Are Here" locator to orient the people who use it to find an employee *and* should not show "private or sensitive" areas in the workplace.

Figure 1.18   Before (left) and after (right) red-tagging.

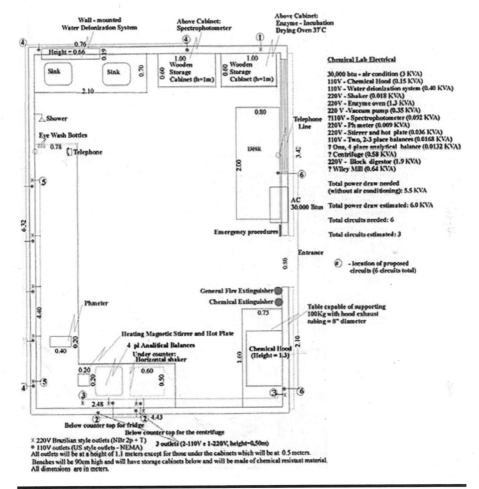

Figure 1.19 Overhead view of a workplace for placing "things." (Source: From http://lba.cptec.inpe.br/lba/eng/infra/stmchemlab2.GIF. With permission.)

Frontal views of a section of a workplace, such as a desk or file cabinet, indicate where "things" are stored for quick retrieval by employees (see Figure 1.21). A good "rule of thumb" is that all documents should be retrievable in 30 seconds or less by employees.

Marks and signs on walls and floors indicate walkways, working areas, storage areas, special use areas, etc. There are two important "mark and sign" methods that promote orderliness: (1) painting strategy and (2) signboard strategy.

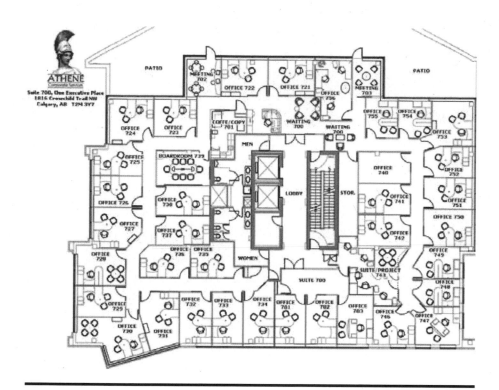

Figure 1.20 Overhead view of a workplace for locating employees. (Source: From http://www.athenecorporate.com/images/Floor_Plan_Large.gif. With permission.)

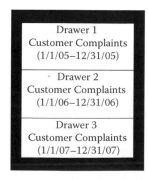

Figure 1.21 Final view of a file cabinet.

Table 1.12   Painting Method for Promoting Orderliness

Category	Subcategory	Color
Paint floors within a work area to indicate the function of a subcategory	Work area	Green
	Rest area	Blue
	Walkway	Orange
Paint lines on the floor within a work area to indicate the function of a subcategory	Opening and closing radius of a door	Yellow broken line
	Direction arrows	Yellow arrows
	Place marker for work in process	White solid line
	Place marker for operations	Corner white lines
	Place marker for defective things	Solid red line
	Place lines over dangerous areas (e.g., wires running over a walkway or a hot motor)	Yellow and black tiger stripe line
Paint lines on the floor between work areas to indicate the separation of the function of a subcategory	Work area boundary	Solid yellow line
	Entrance and exit to a work area	Broken yellow line

The "painting strategy" involves painting different-colored marks and signs on floors and walls to indicate work areas, hazardous areas, rest areas, forklift pathways, walkways, etc. One possible painting strategy for creating orderliness on floors is shown in Table 1.12. Other examples of painting strategies are shown in Figures 1.22 through 1.24.

One final painting strategy for equipment analyzes how equipment is used to develop "set-up and put-away" rules. Set-up and put-away rules pay particular attention to when and how the "things" are picked up and used, which is a primary driver of how and where they are put away. If something is used 50 times a day, then this multiplies the time wasted in finding the item and taking it to where it needs to be used. Labels and names should be standardized. Write labels and other signs clearly so they can be read at an appropriate distance. Ensure that the naming label cannot get lost. Make the item and the storage location match, such as by writing the same name on the item and the storage location. The tool board, as in Figure 1.25, provides a mechanism to store tools by painting their outline on the pegboard.

Figure 1.22 Warehouse view 1.

Figure 1.23 Warehouse view 2. (Source: From http://astrooptics.com/assets/ images/floor_marking_sm.gif. With permission.)

The "signboard strategy" involves the proper placement of inventory and machines in easily identifiable work areas. The signboard strategy works hand in hand with the painting strategy. Table 1.13 shows the structure of a signboard strategy.

Figures 1.26 through 1.28 provide examples of a signboard strategy utilized in a particular work area.

An ***inventory management system*** minimizes the cost of inventory in a work area. The components of a simple inventory system include safety stock, lead-time, reorder level, and order size. Safety stock is the minimum inventory level required

Figure 1.24   Warehouse view 3.

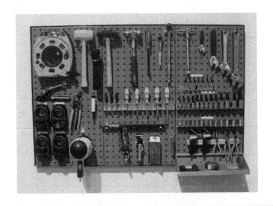

Figure 1.25   Storage board using Seiton. (Source: From http://www.tpslean.com/ images/5s1.jpg. With permission.)

for continuous and safe operation of the workplace. It is a cost of business and is frequently needed to provide satisfactory customer service. However, safety stock must be carefully controlled because it is an expense and a form of waste. Lead-time is the cycle time between when an order for an item is placed and when it is received into inventory. If the lead-time is too long for a given item, then employees may have to begin using safety stock, or even experience a stock-out. Reorder level is the predetermined amount of on-hand inventory that will initiate a reorder. Order size is the number of units ordered when inventory gets to the reorder level.

Table 1.13   Structure for a Signboard Strategy

Categories	Strategy	Method
Work areas	Location of work areas	Overhead (hanging) sign indicating work area
Machines	Location of machine indicator	Overhead sign indicating machine X in work area Y
		On-machine sign indicating work area, machine name, operator
Inventory	Location of inventory	Overhead sign indicating inventory Z in work area Y
		Shelf sign indicating inventory Z in work area Y on shelf A
	Identification of inventory	Sign on inventory item Z with shelf A in work area Y
		Placement lines or colors on shelf A for inventory Z in work area Y
	Quantity of inventory	Lines or colors on shelf A for inventory Z in work area Y that indicates maximum and minimum stacking heights

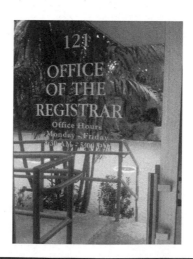

Figure 1.26   Signboard for a work area.

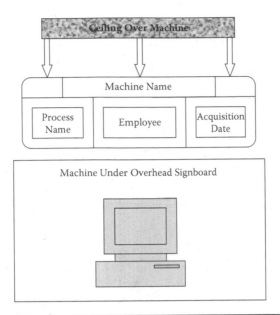

Figure 1.27 Signboard for a machine.

Figure 1.28 Signboard location indicators for inventory. (Source: From http://gembapantarei.com/1.jpg. With permission.)

Inventory not in use is kept in one of two places: (1) a storage area or (2) a "5S" common place (Sarkar, 2006, p. 34). A storage area can be a closet, a file cabinet, a shelf, or a warehouse, to name a few options. A "5S" common place is an area (corner of a store room, shelf, etc.) designated for the placement of excess inventory or red-tagged things that are wanted, but not needed. That is, they are needed less frequently than once a year. Note that if you need an item, check the "5S" common area *before* removing the item from inventory or ordering it from a vendor.

1.2.2.6.1.3 Number 3: Seiso (Spic & Span or Cleaning)

"Seiso" is an attitude that considers a dirty and untidy workplace intolerable. Make cleaning a cultural cornerstone of your organization. Seiso is analogous to personal hygiene for people. A great test of Seiso in the workplace is to visit restrooms. If they are clean, bright, dry, and odor-free, then Seiso may be in the workplace. If they are dirty, dark, damp, and smelly, then Seiso is not in the workplace. Restroom cleanliness is one of the "acid tests" of Seiso.

Cleanliness is accomplished in three phases. In Phase 1, clean everything that involves sweeping, mopping, wiping, and scrubbing floors, equipment, and things. In Phase 2, clean specific items, tools, machines, and workplaces. For example, clean specific sections of machines and check oil levels and ventilation. In Phase 3, clean at the root-cause level. At this level, employees seek out the root causes of grime and dirt, and eliminate them using preventive maintenance (PM). PM is used to ensure that things do not fail or malfunction during normal operation. One can also use the time spent cleaning an item to think about how it can be improved. The perfect item, for example, can be cleaned in a single wipe — or maybe clean itself.

Mental discipline is very important to Seiso. An attitude of cleanliness leads to clean and clear thinking that reflects in all aspects of work.

Before and after photos of Seiso are shown in Figure 1.29 and Figure 1.30, respectively. They display the dramatic effect Seiso can have on the mental health and well-being of employees in the affected workplace.

Figure 1.29 Workplace before Seiso.

Figure 1.30   Workplace after Seiso.

1.2.2.6.1.4 Number 4: Seiketsu (Standardized Cleanup)

"Seiketsu" is the development of an integrated system of "best-practice" methods for Seiri (sorting), Seiton (ordering), and Seiso (cleaning). Seiketsu is used to prevent backsliding in the workplace. It is implemented using two administrative steps:

Step 1: Assign responsibility to employees for "5S" activities in small geographical areas.

Step 2: Integrate "5S" activities into each employee's regular work responsibilities; that is, make standardized cleanup a habit.

In the first step, management assigns responsibility for the "5S"s to the supervisors responsible for each work area in a business. This is best accomplished using an overhead view of a work area; for example, see Figure 1.20. The overhead view of work should clearly indicate who is responsible for the "5S"s in each geographical area. In the second step, management must integrate "5S" activities into each employee's regular responsibilities within their respective work area. All employees define their work (within their geographical work area) as doing *and* "5S"ing their work. This view of work endorses responsibility and accountability by promoting the personal discipline required to adhere to the "5S"s.

Standardized cleanup can be incorporated into the organization's culture by creating key indicators (metrics) that monitor its progress for all work areas by day and for each work area by month. Table 1.14 shows an example of a partial Seiketsu matrix for the workplace shown in Figure 1.20 that can be used to determine the proportion of work areas that are "5S"ed by day (see the right-most column). It can supply the data to construct a p-chart for the proportion of work areas "5S"ed by day; see Figure 1.31. If the proportion of work areas "5S"ed by day is stable, as it is, then a Pareto diagram can be used to identify the problematic work areas for attention by management; see Figure 1.32.

Table 1.14   Partial Seiketsu Matrix for Figure 1.20

| Day | Waiting | | Coffee | | Meeting | | | Percentage of Areas "5S"ed |
	700A	700B	701	Lobby	702	703		
1/1/2007	Y	Y	Y	Y	Y	Y		0
1/2/2007	Y	N	Y	Y	Y	Y		2
1/3/2007	Y	Y	Y	Y	Y	N		3
1/4/2007	Y	Y	Y	Y	Y	Y		0
1/5/2007	Y	Y	Y	Y	Y	Y		2
1/6/2007	Y	Y	Y	Y	Y	Y		1
1/7/2007	Y	Y	Y	Y	Y	Y		0
1/8/2007	Y	Y	Y	Y	Y	Y		2
1/9/2007	Y	Y	Y	Y	Y	Y		2
1/10/2007	Y	Y	Y	Y	Y	Y		0
1/11/2007	Y	Y	Y	Y	Y	N		4
1/12/2007	Y	Y	Y	Y	Y	Y		0
1/13/2007	Y	N	Y	Y	Y	Y		2
1/14/2007	Y	Y	Y	Y	Y	N		3
1/15/2007	Y	Y	Y	Y	Y	Y		0
1/16/2007	Y	Y	Y	Y	Y	Y		2
1/17/2007	Y	Y	Y	Y	Y	Y		1
1/18/2007	Y	Y	Y	Y	Y	Y		0
1/19/2007	Y	Y	Y	Y	Y	Y		2
1/20/2007	Y	Y	Y	Y	Y	Y		2
1/21/2007	Y	Y	Y	Y	Y	Y		0
1/22/2007	Y	N	Y	Y	Y	Y		2
1/23/2007	Y	Y	Y	Y	Y	N		3
1/24/2007	Y	Y	Y	Y	Y	Y		0
1/25/2007	Y	Y	Y	Y	Y	Y		2
1/26/2007	Y	Y	Y	Y	Y	Y		1

Table 1.14   Partial Seiketsu Matrix for Figure 1.20 (continued)

	Waiting		Coffee		Meeting			Percentage of Areas "5S"ed
Day	700A	700B	701	Lobby	702	703		
1/27/2007	Y	Y	Y	Y	Y	Y		0
1/28/2007	Y	Y	Y	Y	Y	Y		2
1/29/2007	Y	Y	Y	Y	Y	Y		2
1/30/2007	Y	Y	Y	Y	Y	N		3
1/31/2007	Y	Y	Y	Y	Y	Y		0
Number of days each area not "5S"ed	0	3	0	0	0	5		43

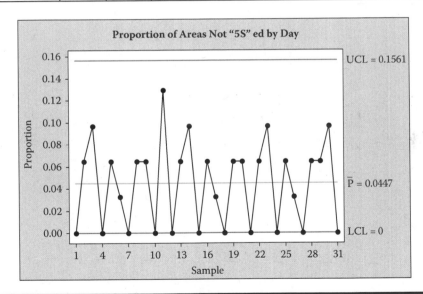

Figure 1.31   p-Chart of "5S" process.

As one can see from the Pareto diagram in Figure 1.32, seven of the 49 work areas (726, 773, 746, 703, 704, 780, and 708) account for 100 percent of the non "5S"ed areas. That is, 14.3 percent of the work areas account for 100 percent of the non-"5S"ed areas. Team members can now focus on these areas and try to identify the barriers to the "5S" techniques, with the hopes of implementing the "5S"s across the entire organization.

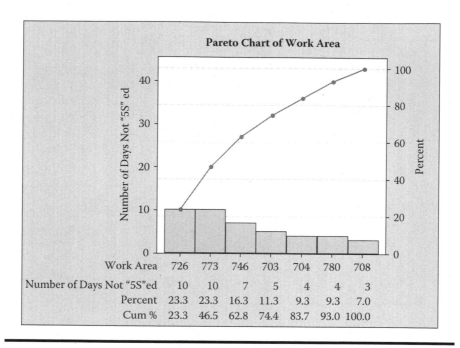

Figure 1.32   Pareto diagram of work areas not "5S"ed.

1.2.2.6.1.5 Number 5: Shitsuke (Personal Discipline)

"Shitsuke" makes a habit of the first "4S"s by forging them into a complete systemic disciplined approach to management. Perhaps the most important thing a manager can do to encourage his or her subordinates to take a disciplined approach to work is to model the desired behavior. Your workers will listen to you when you tell them how they should behave, and they will watch carefully to see if you are following your own advice. Failure to do so leads to a cynical workforce.

Professional management assumes the existence of personal discipline (accountability and responsibility) in the workplace. Without it, the "5S"s and Lean Six Sigma cannot be effective forms of management. Personal discipline begins with top management and cascades throughout an organization through hiring, training, and supervisory policies and procedures. Do not expect the workforce to exhibit personal discipline if top management does not practice it.

The path to personal discipline goes through four steps. The first step is unconscious incompetence. In this step, a worker bee is unaware of his job and "5S" responsibilities and accountabilities, and consequently, performs his job and the "5S"s with variable success. The second step is conscious incompetence. Here, a worker bee is aware of his job and "5S" responsibilities and accountabilities, but is not able to perform his job and the "5S"s with a high success rate. This is a frustrating work experience. The third step is conscious competence. In this step, a worker bee is aware of his job and "5S" responsibilities and accountabilities, and is able to perform his job and the "5S"s with a high success rate with conscious effort. The fourth step is unconscious competence. Here, a worker bee understands his job and "5S" responsibilities and accountabilities, and without conscious effort performs his job and the "5S"s with a high success rate. The "5S"s are the vehicle for all employees — top management through worker bees — to practice the improvement of their personal discipline skills.

1.2.2.6.2 Housekeeping: Step 2

The second step of housekeeping is accomplished using the Standardize–Do–Study–Act (SDSA) cycle which is a method that helps worker bees acquire process knowledge through standardizing the processes that define their jobs. It includes four steps:

1. *Standardize:* worker bees study the processes that define their jobs and develop best-practice methods (flowcharts), with key indicators. It is important for all employees doing a job to agree on the best-practice method for the job. If multiple employees perform the same job differently, there will be increased variation in output and problems will result for the customer (customers) of those outputs.
2. *Do:* worker bees use the best-practice methods on a trial basis for a limited period of time while collecting data on the standardized processes' key indicators (metrics); this is an experiment.
3. *Study:* worker bees analyze the data on the key indicators to determine the effectiveness of the best-practice method.
4. *Act*: managers establish the standardized best-practice method and formalize it through training.

For example, the Medical Records Department in a hospital receives, processes, and files patients' medical records. The key objective is to file more than 80 percent of all medical records within 30 days of a patient's checking out of the hospital. This is a legally mandated objective. The key indicator is percent of medical records filed within 30 days of a patient checking out of the hospital by month.

The director of the Medical Records Department decided to standardize the medical records process. Before standardization of this process, the percentage of medical record filed within 30 days of a patient leaving the hospital was a predictable process with an average of 22 percent per month that would rarely go above 32 percent per month or below 12 percent per month. Recall that the process should never drop below 80 percent of medical records files in a given month. The SDSA cycle was applied to the Medical Records Department. It is described below.

Standardize: The director standardized the medical records process in three steps. First, she trained all her worker bees on how to construct a flowchart. Second, she asked each worker bee to create a detailed flowchart of the medical records process. Third, she reviewed all the flowcharts with her entire staff and created one best-practice flowchart. The best-practice flowchart incorporated all the strengths and eliminated all the weaknesses of each worker bee's flowchart.

Do: Worker bees use the best-practice methods on a trial basis for a limited period of time while collecting data on the standardized processes' key indicators (metrics). In the case of the Medical Records Department, the director collected baseline data on the key indicator for a period of months.

Study: Worker bees analyzed data on the key indicators to determine the effectiveness of the best-practice methods. Again, in the case of the Medical Records Department, the director studied the key indicator data and determined that the percentage of medical records filed within 30 days of a patient leaving the hospital after standardization was a predictable process with an average of 30 percent per month that would rarely go above 38 percent per month or below 22 percent per month. She knew that this was still woefully inadequate given her state-mandated key objective.

Act: Managers establish the standardized best-practice method and formalize it through training. In the case of the Medical Records Department, the director formalized the best-practice method by training all worker bees in the method and putting it in the department's training manual for the training of all future employees.

Process knowledge was acquired by standardizing the process, thereby paving the way for the future acquisition of more knowledge. The director of the Medical Records department continued to work on increasing the percentage of medical record files within 30 days of the patient leaving the hospital.

1.2.2.6.3 Complexity

Complexity frequently increases the incidence of non-value-added steps in a process. Recall that one of the major sources of complexity is the special cause reaction to common causes of variation, called "tampering with a process." This may be why the IRS Code is so convoluted, or everyone must take off their shoes when going through security at the airport.

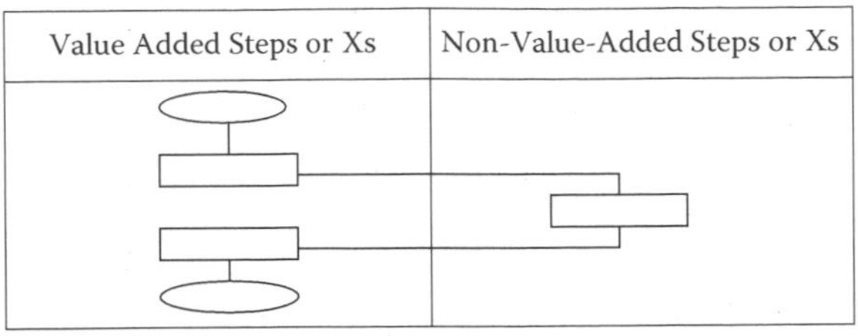

Value Added Steps or Xs	Non-Value-Added Steps or Xs

Figure 1.33   VA/NVA generic flowchart.

As discussed previously in this book, non-value-added steps in a process include any step that (1) customers are not willing to pay for; (2) do not change the product or service; (3) contain errors, defects, or omissions; (4) require preparation or setup; (5) involve control or inspection; (6) involve over-production, special processing, and inventory; or (6) involve waiting and delays. Value-added steps include steps that customers are willing to pay for because they positively change the product or service in the view of the customer.

Figure 1.33 shows a generic flowchart constructed to highlight value-added (VA) and non-value-added (NVA) steps in a process. VA/NVA flowcharts are used to identify non-value-added steps in a process for possible elimination or modification, thereby reducing the complexity of a process.

Example. Imagine a flowchart of a data entry process; see Figure 1.34. The process starts when a data entry operator clocks into work at 9:00 a.m. First, she or he determines if there is a data processing job that was not completed the prior day. If yes, she or he turns on the computer and brings up the necessary programs. If no, she or he picks up datasets for data entry, then turns on the computer and brings up the necessary programs. Second, she or he determines if the current data entry job requires verification. If no, she or he enters the dataset into the appropriate database. If yes, she or he enters the dataset into the appropriate database and verifies the dataset (for accuracy). If there are errors detected during verification, then she or he corrects the errors and re-verifies the data. If there are no errors, she or he alerts the dataset owner that the data has been entered into the appropriate database. Next, she or he looks at the clock and determines if it is 5:00 p.m. If not, then she or he picks up another dataset for entry into a database. If yes, then she or he turns off the computer and clocks out.

The flowchart in Figure 1.34 can be redrawn as a VA/NVA flowchart; see Figure 1.35.

As one can see from Figure 1.35, correcting errors is a non-value-added step; that is, customers do not want to pay for extra processing; they want it correct the first time. Interestingly, verifying the dataset may be a necessary non-value-added step. In this case, it is not clear whether inspection (verification) adds value to the data entry operation. If the proportion of data entries is low, the cost of fixing a data entry error is high, and the cost of a data entry slipping through is low, then

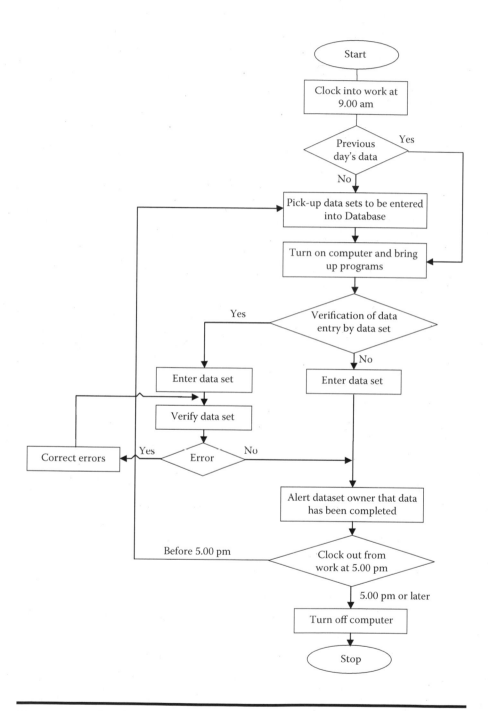

Figure 1.34   Flowchart of a data entry process.

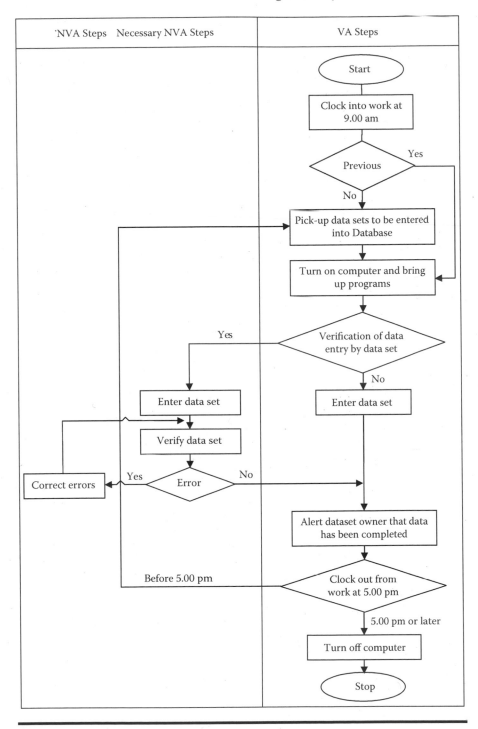

Figure 1.35 VA/NVA flowchart of a data entry process.

verification is a non-value-added step. However, if the proportion of data entries is high, the cost of fixing a data entry error is low, and the cost of a data entry slipping through is high, then verification is a necessary non-value-added step. To better understand the logic of the two previous sentences, read Deming's "kp rule"; see Gitlow and Levine (2004).

1.2.2.6.3.1 Optional Reading

W. Edwards Deming developed the "kp rule" for determining the economic viability of an inspection point (see Deming, 1986). It states that, given a stable process, there are only two alternatives for inspection: (1) no inspection or (2) 100 percent inspection. This rule is used to minimize the total cost of incoming and intermediate materials, final products, and repairing and testing those products that fail. The assumptions for the use of the "kp rule" are not restrictive and are applicable to many common situations.

The following notation is necessary to determine when to do 100 percent inspection and when to do no inspection:

p = the average incoming fraction of defective items in incoming lots of items. It is easily obtained from daily quality control (QC) metrics. The kp rule assumes that the process under study is stable with an average incoming fraction of defective items, called "p"

k_1 = the cost to initially inspect one item

k_2 = the cost to dismantle, repair, reassemble, and test a good or service that fails because a defective item was used in its production

If a process is stable around the fraction, p, the "kp rule" states:

1. If k_1/k_2 is greater than p, then do no inspection. That is, no inspection is the policy that minimizes the total cost. This occurs if the fraction of incoming defective items, p, is very low, the cost of inspecting an incoming item is high, and the cost of the defective item getting into production is low; therefore, no inspection is needed. The rationale is that there is little risk or penalty associated with incoming defective items.
2. If k_1/k_2 is less than or equal to p, then do 100 percent inspection. That is, 100 percent inspection is the policy that minimizes the total cost. This occurs if the fraction of incoming defective items, p, is high, the cost of inspecting an incoming item is low, and the cost of the defective item getting into production is high; therefore, 100 percent inspection is needed. The rationale here is that there is great risk and penalty attached to incoming defective items.

It is important to note that "no inspection" does not mean the absence of information. Small samples should always be drawn from every lot, or on a skip-lot basis, for information about the process under study; that is on "p." This information should be recorded on control charts to facilitate process improvement. Note that this information is *not* used to sort good items from bad items (inspection); rather, it is used to provide the information to calculate "p" for the "kp rule."

The "kp rule" is appropriate between any two points in a process, be they between a supplier and the firm, between internal process steps, or between the firm and a customer.

Example. A car manufacturer is deciding whether to purchase $25 million of equipment that would test engines purchased from vendors (see Deming, 1986, pp. 420–422). The vendor's process is stable. The following figures have been determined:

- On average, 1 in 150 incoming engines is defective ($p = 1/150 = 0.0067$).
- The inspection cost to screen out incoming defective engines is $50 per engine ($k_1 = \$50$).
- The cost for corrective action if a defective engine gets into production is $500 per defective engine ($k_2 = \$500$).

Consequently, $k_1/k_2 = 50/500 = 0.1$. Note that 0.1 is greater than 0.0067. Therefore, k_1/k_2 is greater than "p," and the correct course of action would be to do no initial inspection on incoming engines to achieve minimum total cost.

If no engines are inspected, the auto company would expect to incur the $500 cost in 1 out of 150 engines. This translates into an average corrective action cost of $3.33 per engine ($500 \times 1/150$). By eliminating initial inspection, the company would save $46.67 per engine ($50 – $3.33) on average. As the company purchases 4000 engines per day, this translates into a daily savings of $186,680 ($4000 \times$ $46.67), plus the savings of the interest on borrowing $25 million for testing equipment (about $13,000 per day at the time), and time freed up to work on improving quality. So, doing no inspection saved the company about $52,000,000 per year. The next step in the pursuit of quality is for the auto company to work with its engine vendor to reduce the fraction of defective engines (see Deming, 1986, p. 420–422).

1.2.2.7 Principle 7

Recall Principle 7: effective communication requires operational definitions. I punctuate the importance of operational definitions with another example (see Deming, 1986, p. 27.7). A firm produces washers. One of the critical quality characteristics is roundness. The following procedure is one way to arrive at an operational definition of roundness, as long as the buyer and seller agree on it.

Step 1: Criterion for roundness:
    Buyer: "Use calipers that are in reasonably good order." (You perceive at once the need to question every word.)
    Seller: "What is 'reasonably good order'?" (We settle the question by letting you use your calipers.)

Seller: "But how should I use them?"

Buyer: "We'll be satisfied if you just use them in the usual way."

Seller: "At what temperature?"

Buyer: "The temperature of this room."

Buyer: "Take six measures of the diameter about 30° apart. Record the results."

Seller: "But what is 'about 30° apart'? Don't you mean exactly 30°?"

Buyer: "No, there's no such thing as exactly 30° in the physical world. So try for 30°. We'll be satisfied."

Buyer: "If the range between the six diameters doesn't exceed 0.007 centimeters, we'll declare the washer to be round." (They have determined the criterion for roundness.)

Step 2: Test of roundness:

Select a particular washer.

Take the six measurements and record the results in centimeters: 3.365, 3.363, 3.368, 3.366, 3.366, and 3.369.

The range is 3.369 to 3.363, or a 0.006 difference. They test for conformance by comparing the range of 0.006 with the criterion range of 0.007 (*Step 1*).

Step 3: Decision on roundness:

Because the range in diameters is less than 0.007 centimeters, they declare it to be round.

If a buyer and seller of a quality characteristic agree on an operational definition of the quality characteristic, then many of their potential problems will disappear.

1.2.2.8 Principle 8

Recall Principle 8: expansion of knowledge requires theory. The Plan–Do–Study–Act (PDSA) cycle is the major tool of Total Quality Management (TQM) for expanding knowledge by continuously improving the theory about a process. The DMAIC, DMADV, and Lean models are the major tools of Lean Six Sigma management for expanding knowledge by continuous improvement or innovation of the theory about a process.

1.2.2.8.1 PDSA Cycle

The PDSA cycle can aid employees in improving and innovating processes and thereby acquiring process knowledge, by reducing the difference between customers' needs (called Voice of the Customer) and process performance (called Voice of the Process). The PDSA cycle consists of four stages: Plan, Do, Study, and Act. Initially, a plan is developed to improve or innovate the standardized best-practice flowchart developed using the SDSA cycle. The revised best-practice method is characterized by a revised flowchart. Hence, a process improvement team *plans*

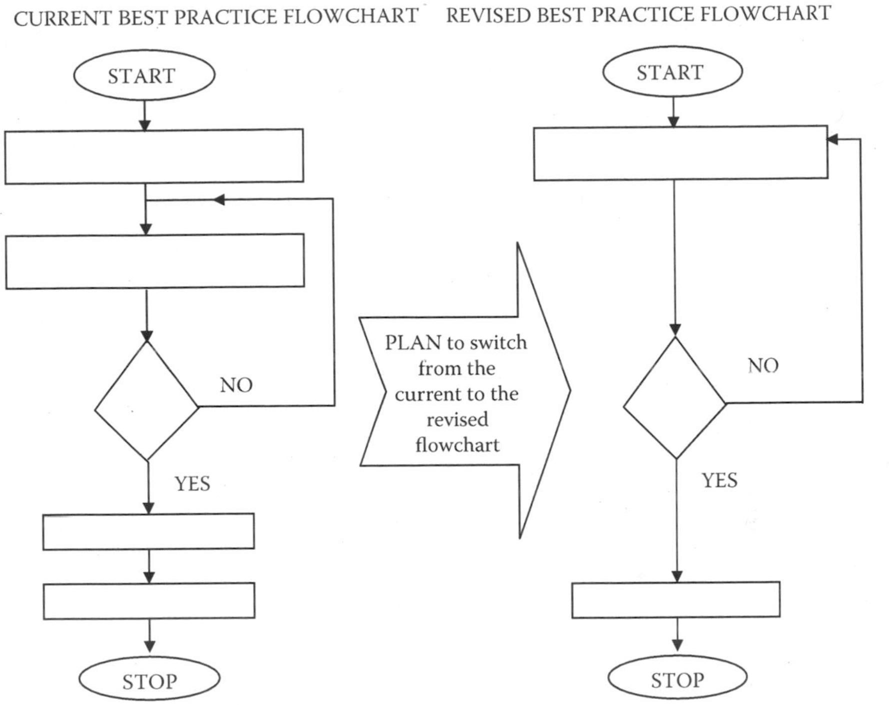

CURRENT BEST PRACTICE FLOWCHART   REVISED BEST PRACTICE FLOWCHART

Figure 1.36   PLAN portion of the PDSA cycle.

to modify a process from operating under the current best-practice flowchart to operating under a revised (and improved or innovated) best-practice flowchart, as shown in Figure 1.36.

The revised best practice flowchart is identified using four possible methods:

1. Statistically analyzing key indicator data on the components of the process under study to identify an effective change concept is the acquisition of knowledge. In the case of the Medical Records Department, cycle time data was collected for the length of time from when a physician ordered a medical report until the medical records department received (in the inbox) the patient's medical report, from each of 16 departments, such as EEG, EKG, and Laboratory. Statistical analysis showed that 15 of the 16 departments' cycle times were stable and predictable processes with cycle times being measured in hours. However, the Laboratory Department had cycle times being measured in weeks, with an average of six weeks. From this analysis, it was obvious that a huge proportion of medical records could not be filed within 30 days if one of the component reports took an average of six weeks. The director of the Medical Records Department went to the Laboratory Department and was greeted by the director with the comment: "We grow cultures and

they can't be rushed." The director of the Medical Records Department asked if she could visit the Laboratory Department anyway. The Laboratory director agreed. After poking around the lab, the Medical Records director noticed that each lab report required three signatures before it could be released. She asked the first signer how often he refused to sign a lab report. He replied never. She asked the second signer how often he refused to sign a lab report. The second signer had seen the director's interaction with the first signer and said: "It happens." She asked: "Does it happen every day?" He said: "No." She asked: "Every week?" He said: "No." She asked: "Every month?" He said: "No." She asked: "Every quarter?" He said: "No." She asked: "Every year?" He said: "No." The director of Medical Records asked the director of the Laboratory if he would eliminate the need for the two signatures because they were no screen for quality. The Laboratory director agreed with a modicum of irritation. This is the PLAN stage of the PDSA cycle. The revised process was implemented as a pilot test. This is the DO stage of the PDSA cycle. The average cycle time for the laboratory reports fell from 6 to 3.75 weeks. The percentage of medical records filed on time rose from an average of 30 percent to an average of 55 percent. This was better but still woefully inadequate for the state-mandated goal of 80 percent per month. This is the STUDY stage of the PDSA cycle. Finally, the new or modified plan, which is the acquisition of process knowledge, is formalized through training. This is the ACT stage of the PDSA cycle.

2. Benchmarking your process against another organization's process, which is considered excellent to identify an effective change concept. The other organization should be one that is known for the quality of the process under study. Benchmarking is accomplished by comparing your flowchart with another organization's flowchart to determine if anything in their flowchart makes sense in your organization. If it does, utilize the new information to improve your flowchart. This is the acquisition of process knowledge. For example, a call center can benchmark its customer complaint resolution process flowchart with a retail store's customer complaint resolution process flowchart.

3. Utilizing a list of 70 tried and proven improvement concepts (see Gitlow, Oppenheim, Oppenheim, and Levine, 2004) to identify an effective change concept. Identifying and utilizing one or more of the 70 change concepts is the acquisition of knowledge. Recall the example of a Student Accounts Office at a major university that experienced an increase, from 10 to 54 percent, in the average percentage of abandoned telephone calls made by students in a one-month period. The cause was identified as the reassignment of three of the department's seven personnel, with no budget to replace them. Subsequently, the department manager turned to the list of 70 change concepts for ideas on how to deal with his situation. The list generated several potentially valuable change concepts, one of which was shift demand. Team members asked themselves: "What is the average number of calls made per student by year?"

The answer was about ten calls per student per year*. Next, they asked: "Does everyone call about ten times per year, or do most people call zero times and a few call 100 times?" The answer was the second scenario. Team members decided that they could use the shift demand strategy by employing the following method. Every time a student calls the Student Accounts Office, his or her social security number is entered into a database. If the number of calls from a particular student exceeds eight in one month, one of the students that calls 100 times per year has been identified. Then, instead of waiting for these frequent callers to call and clog the system during the busiest hours, the Student Accounts Office staff calls the frequent caller at 8:00 a.m. or 6:00 p.m., whether or not they called the office that day, and says: "We know you have been having trouble with your student account; you have called many times; we will stay on the phone with you now until your problem is completely resolved." This shifted the demand from the most constrained time period to the least constrained time period. The percentage of abandoned calls fell dramatically to about 18 percent from its previous level of 54 percent. More Lean Six Sigma efforts further reduced the percentage of abandoned calls to 8 percent, less than the original percent of abandoned calls, with three fewer employees. This is the acquisition of process knowledge.

4. Studying the available literature or speaking with experts about the process to identify helpful change concepts is the acquisition of knowledge. Libraries, the Internet, and experts are fantastic sources of change concepts. For example, a worker was having a difficult time with a boss who demanded too much work in too short a time frame. She went to the Internet and searched the "difficult boss" literature. She identified a change concept that she thought might help her. The concept was simply to ask the boss who just demanded work product "right away," if one week was an acceptable interpretation of "right away." It turned out that it was and the worker's problem was resolved to both parties' satisfaction. This is the acquisition of process knowledge.

To summarize, the PLAN (revised flowchart) is tested using an experiment on a small scale or trial basis (DO) for a predetermined period of time, the effects of the plan are studied using measurements from key indicators (STUDY), and appropriate corrective actions are taken and locked in with training and documentation (ACT). The PDSA cycle continues forever in an uphill progression of continuous improvement.

Another application of the PDSA cycle to acquire process knowledge (developing theory) can be shown by developing a theory to predict the next number in the following sequence of numbers: 5, 8, ?. (Personal conversation with Lloyd Provost, API)

---

* The author apologizes for not remembering the exact average number of calls per year. Fortunately, the actual number does not affect the value of the example.

PLAN: My theory is that the difference between the two numbers is 3, so the next number is 11.

DO: I predict 11.

STUDY: The next number is 13.

ACT: I reject my theory and go back to the PLAN stage.

PLAN: My revised theory is that the difference between the 5 and 8 is 3, and the difference between 8 and 13 is 5, so the difference between the next two numbers will be 7, so I predict, 20.

DO: I predict 20.

STUDY: The next number is 21.

ACT: I reject my theory and go back to the PLAN stage.

PLAN: My revised theory is that the next number is the sum of the previous two numbers, so I predict 34.

DO: I predict 34.

STUDY: The next number is 34.

ACT: I tentatively give my theory credibility and submit it to another test.

PLAN: My revised theory is that the next number is the sum of the previous two numbers, so I predict 55.

DO: I predict 55.

STUDY: The next number is 55.

ACT: I give my theory more credibility and submit it to another test.

PLAN: My revised theory is that the next number can be predicted using a Fibonacci sequence, that is, the sum of the previous two numbers [0, 1, 1, 2, 3, 5, 8, 13, 21, 34, 55, 89, ..., ...], so I predict 89.

DO: I predict 89.

STUDY: The next number is 89.

ACT: Wow, I realize that the stream of numbers is the Fibonacci sequence. I give my Fibonacci sequence theory more credibility and submit it to another test, and on and on.

1.2.2.8.2 Empowerment

"Empowerment" is a term commonly used by managers in today's organizational environment. Currently, the prevailing definition of empowerment relies loosely on the notion of dropping decision making down to the lowest appropriate level in an organization. Empowerment's basic premise is that if people are given the authority to make decisions, they will take pride in their work, be willing to take risks, and work harder to make things happen. While this sounds ideal, frequently employees are empowered until they make a mistake, and then the hatchet falls. Most employees know this and treat the popular definition of empowerment without too much respect. Consequently, empowerment in its current form is destructive to Lean Six Sigma management.

Empowerment in a Lean Six Sigma sense has a different aim and definition. The aim is to increase "joy in work" for all employees through the acquisition and application of process knowledge. The definition follows.

Empowerment is a process that provides worker bees with the:

1. Opportunity to define and document their jobs (key processes)
2. Opportunity to learn about their work (processes) through training and development
3. Opportunity to work toward improvement and innovation of the best-practice methods that make up their work (processes) using the PDSA cycle (acquisition and application of process knowledge)
4. Latitude to use judgment to make decisions within the context of best-practice methods
5. Environment of trust in which superiors will not react negatively to the latitude taken by worker bees in decision making within the context of a best-practice method

Empowerment starts with executives, but it requires the commitment of all employees. Executives need to provide employees with all five of the preceding conditions. Item (5) above requires that any negative results emanating from an employee using his or her judgment within the context of a best-practice method lead to improvement or innovation of the best-practice method — and not to judgment and punishment of the employee.

Worker bees need to accept responsibility for:

1. Increasing their training and knowledge of their work (the system)
2. Participating in the development, standardization, improvement, and innovation of best-practice methods that make up their jobs (the process)
3. Increasing their latitude in decision making within the context of best-practice methods

Worker bees must be educated to understand that increased variability in output will result if each worker follows his own best-practice method. For example, if five customer-service representatives all deal with a hostile customer in different ways, it will increase the variability in the customer's resulting attitude. Worker bees learn how to reach consensus on the best-practice method for a given task. Management should understand the differences between worker bees and channel these differences into the development of the best-practice method in a constructive manner.

Note that latitude to make decisions within the context of a best-practice method refers to the options a worker bee has in resolving problems within the confines of a best-practice method, not to modification of the best-practice method. Differentiating between the need to change the best-practice method and latitude within the context of the best-practice method must take place at the operational level.

Teams must work to improve or to innovate best-practice methods. Individuals can also work to improve or to innovate best-practice methods; however, the efforts of individuals must be shared with and approved by the team. Empowerment can only exist in an environment of trust that supports planned experimentation concerning ideas for improvement or innovation of best-practice methods. Ideas for improvement and innovation can come from individuals or from the team, but the test of an idea's worthiness must be conducted through planned experiments by the team. Anything else will result in chaos because everybody will just "do his own thing."

Empowerment is made operational at two levels. First, employees are empowered to develop and document a best-practice method using the SDSA cycle. Second, employees are empowered to work on the improvement or innovation of a best-practice method through application of the PDSA cycle.

1.2.2.8.3 DMAIC Model

The DMAIC model is the Lean Six Sigma alternative to the PDSA cycle for improving an existing process, product, or service. DMAIC is an acronym for Define–Measure–Analyze–Improve–Control. An accounting report example will be used to illustrate the DMAIC model (see Friedman and Gitlow, 2002).

Define Phase. The Define Phase involves (1) preparing a business charter (rationale for the project); (2) understanding the relationships between Suppliers–Inputs–Processes–Outputs–Customers (called SIPOC analysis); (3) analyzing Voice of the Customer data to identify the critical-to-quality (CTQs) characteristics important to customers; and (4) developing a project objective.

A Lean Six Sigma team was assigned by top management to review the cycle time for the preparation of a monthly report by the Accounting Department as a potential Lean Six Sigma project. This involved identifying the need for the project (relative to other potential projects), the costs and benefits of the project, the resources required for the project, and the timeframe of the project. As a consequence of performing a SIPOC analysis and a Voice of the Customer analysis, the team determined that management wants the monthly accounting report completed in seven days (the desired [nominal] time is seven days). The team also determined that the report should never be completed in less than four days (the relevant information is not available before then) and never more than ten days (the report is required for decision-making purposes). Team members identified the project objective as follows:

> Reduce (direction) the variability in the cycle time (measure or critical-to-quality, CTQ) to produce an error-free accounting report (process) from the current level of 7 ± 3 days to 7 ± 1.5 days (target) by January 10, 2007 (deadline).

Measure Phase. The Measure Phase involves (1) developing operational definitions for each CTQ variable; (2) determining the validity of the measurement system for the CTQs; and (3) establishing baseline capabilities for each CTQ.

Let us return to the accounting report example. First, the team members created an operational definition of variability in cycle time such that all relevant personnel agreed on the definition. For example, they clearly identified the start and stop points needed to compute cycle time. Second, they performed a measurement systems analysis to determine the ability of the measurement system to properly measure "variability in cycle time." Finally, the members of the team collected baseline data about variability in cycle time and statistically analyzed it to get a clear picture of the current situation.

Analyze Phase. The Analyze Phase involves identifying the upstream variables (Xs) for each CTQ using a flowchart. Upstream variables are the factors (Xs) that affect the performance of a CTQ. Additionally, the Analyze Phase involves using Failure Modes and Effects Analysis (FMEA) to eliminate Xs that are not likely to impact the CTQ; operationally define each X; collect baseline data for each X; perform studies to determine the ability of the measurement system for each X to adequately reflect the behavior of each X; establish baseline capabilities for each X; and understand the effect of each X on each CTQ.

Again, referring back to the accounting report example, team members identify all input and system variables (called the Xs) that impact the CTQ (variability in cycle time) using a flowchart. These Xs are:

X_1 = number of days from request to receipt for line item A data
X_2 = number of days from request to receipt for line item B data
X_3 = number of days from request to receipt for line item C data
X_4 = number of days from request to receipt for line item D data
X_5 = number of days to reformat the line item data to prepare the report
X_6 = number of days to prepare the report
X_7 = accounting clerk preparing the report (Mary or Joe)

X_8 = number of errors in the report
X_9 = number of days to correct the report
X_{10} = accounting supervisor performing the corrections to the report (Harry or Sue)
X_{11} = number of signatures required before the report is released

For example, the number of signatures required before releasing the report (X_{11}) may affect the average time to process the report; or the accounting clerk preparing the report (X_7) may dramatically affect the variability in cycle time to produce the report. Next, team members operationally define the Xs and perform measurement systems studies to determine the validity of the measurement systems. Fourth, team members collect baseline data to determine the current status of each X using control charts. Finally, team members study the data and develop hypotheses about the relationships between the Xs and each CTQ. In this case, histograms of the CTQ broken out for each level of each X indicated that X_1 (number of days from request to receipt for line item A data), X_3 (number of days from request to receipt for line item C data), X_7 (accounting clerk preparing the report (Mary or Joe)), and X_{10} (accounting supervisor performing the corrections to the report (Harry or Sue)) may be important to the reduction of variability in the cycle time (CTQ). The other Xs did not substantially affect the CTQ.

Improve Phase. The Improve Phase involves (1) designing experiments to understand the relationships between the CTQs and the Xs; (2) determining the levels of the critical Xs that optimize the CTQs; (3) developing action plans to formalize the level of the Xs that optimize the CTQs; and (4) conducting a pilot test of the revised process using the levels of the critical Xs that will hypothetically optimize the CTQs.

In the accounting report example, team members conducted an experiment to identify the levels of the critical Xs identified in the Analyze Phase to minimize variation in the time to produce the accounting report. The experiment revealed that team members had to work with the personnel responsible for line items A and C to decrease the average and standard deviation of days to forward the line items to the department preparing the report. Further, the experiment revealed that there is an interaction between the clerk preparing the report and the supervisor correcting the report. The analysis showed that if Mary prepared the report, it was best for Sue to correct the report; if Joe prepared the report, it was best for Harry to correct the report. A pilot run of the revised system to produce the accounting report showed a predictable distribution of days to produce the report with a mean of 7 days, a maximum of 8.5 days, and a minimum of 5.5 days.

Control Phase. The Control Phase involves (1) avoiding potential problems with the Xs with risk management and mistake proofing (discussed in the next paragraph); (2) standardizing successful process revisions; (3) controlling the critical Xs; (4) creating a set of instructions for turning the improved process over to the process owner, called a control plan; (5) turning the revised process over to the process owner for continuous turning of the PDSA cycle; and (6) disbanding the team and celebrating its success.

Risk management involves minimizing the potential risks caused by the optimal levels of the critical Xs identified in the Improve Phase. This type of risk is called "collateral damage." Collateral damages are the unanticipated negative effects caused by the optimal settings of the Xs established in the Improve Phase. For example, the optimal levels of the Xs are illegal (violate a regulation) or dangerous (can cause an explosion). Mistake proofing involves installing processes or methods that have a low probability of causing failure modes for the optimal levels of the Xs established in the Improve Phase.

One final time, we return to the accounting report example. Team members identify potential problems, and methods to avoid them, with X_1, X_3, X_7, and X_{10} using risk management and mistake-proofing techniques. For example, they establish procedures to ensure the coupling of clerks and supervisors (and work on resolving problems with the other pairing of workers and supervisors), as well as data collection methods to identify and resolve future problems in the reporting process. The new process is standardized and fully documented in training manuals. At this point, team members turn the revised process over to the process owner, disband, and celebrate their success. The process owner continues to turn the PDSA cycle to achieve a distribution of days to produce the report that is a stable and predictable normal distribution with an average of 7 days, a maximum less than 8.5 days, and a minimum more than 5.5 days.

1.2.2.8.4 DMADV Model

The DMADV model is the Design for Lean Six Sigma (DFSS) model used to create major new features of existing products, services, or processes, or to create entirely new products, services, or processes (see Gitlow, Levine, and Popovich, 2006). It has five phases: Define, Measure, Analyze, Design, and Verify/Validate. Each phase is briefly described below using an example of designing a new dormitory at the University of Miami (see Johnson, Widener, Gitlow, and Popovich 2006).

Define Phase. The Define Phase of the DMADV model has five components: establishing the background and business case, assessing the risks and benefits of the project, forming the team, developing the project plan, and writing the project objective.

The University of Miami has become a strong, private, doctoral-granting university with academic integrity. Rapid growth in student enrollment, a policy that stipulates that all incoming freshmen must live on campus (unless they live with their families), and the wish of the president for a more residential campus, created more demand than supply for on-campus housing. A Design for Lean Six Sigma project team was assembled to develop the business case and project charter for building a new residential dormitory on campus.

The project charter is: To create a design for a high-class living facility that encourages learning and community (product) aimed at executives-in-residence, MBA students, as well as junior and senior undergraduate business students (market segments) to increase (direction) the number of on campus residents (measure of success) by 280 students (target) by July 15, 2008 (deadline). The project leaders were Scott Widener (Master Black Belt) and Adam Johnson (Black Belt).

Measure Phase. The Measure Phase of a Design for Lean Six Sigma project has three steps: (1) segmenting the market, (2) designing and conducting a survey of stakeholder segments, and (3) using the survey results as Quality Function Deployment (QFD) inputs to find CTQ characteristics. QFD is a method team members can use to understand the relationships between the needs and wants of stakeholders and the features of the product, service, or process design.

In the dormitory example, the Dean of the School of Business Administration identified three distinct market segments for the new on-campus housing. These market segments are (1) executives-in-residence, (2) regular MBA students, and (3) junior and senior undergraduate business students. Executives-in-residence are individuals who come to campus for one or two weeks to attend a concentrated class. Currently, no regular MBA students live on campus. Team members developed a survey using the features identified from focus groups. The survey was then completed by a sample of regular MBA and undergraduate business students. Table 1.15 shows the results of the survey broken down by market segment.

Next, team members created a QFD table, crossing the needs and wants of stakeholders (rows) from the survey with the dormitory features (columns); see Table 1.16. The bottom of Table 1.16 indicates the importance of each feature (column) to the stakeholders' needs (row) for the dormitory; for example, simple occupancy rooms is the most important feature (normalized weight = 6.46 percent).

Analyze Phase. The Analyze Phase contains four steps: (1) design generation, (2) design analysis, (3) risk analysis, and (4) model design. The aim of these four steps in the Analyze Phase is to develop high-level designs that surpass customer needs and wants. In addition to this, the designs will be evaluated using risk analysis. Finally, nominal (desired) values are established for all CTQs (features) in the Analyze Phase for the "best" design.

Five room designs were developed in the Analyze Phase:

1. *Undergraduate Preferences:* includes only the features that are deemed "One-Way," "Attractive," or "Must-Be" via the undergraduate responses in the survey.
2. *Graduate Preferences:* includes only the features that are deemed as "One-Way," "Attractive," or "Must-Be" via the graduate responses in the survey.
3. *Eaton Hall:* includes only the features of the nicest dormitory rooms currently available on campus.
4. *Business Suite:* includes only the features and services that have large contributions to business student education.
5. *Luxury Suite:* includes all the features that were deemed "One-Way," "Attractive," or "Must-Be" by any of the market segments via the survey.

Table 1.15   Survey Results Broken Down by Market Segment

Dormitory Features	Freshman Quality Category	Sophomore Quality Category	Junior Quality Category	Senior Quality Category	Undergraduate Composite Quality Category	Graduate Quality Category
Single Occupancy Rooms	O	O	M	O	O	M
Individual Bathrooms	O	A	A	A	A	A
Queen Size Bed	A	A	A	A	A	A
Broadband Internet	A	A	A	O	A	A
Integrated Audio System	A	I	I	I	I	I
Integrated Headphone Jacks	I	I	I	A	I	I
Television	A	A	I	I	A	A
Telephone	A	A	I	M	A	M
Cordless Telephone	A	A	I	A	A	I
Additional Phone Services	A	A	I	A	A	A
Personal Computer Rental Service	I	I	I	A	A	I
Shared Common Printer	A	A	I	A	A	A
Large Corner Desk	A	I	A	A	A	A
Executive Desk Chair	A	I	I	A	A	A
Additional Desk Chairs	A	I	I	A	I	A
Climate Control by Room	M	M	M	M	M	M
Full-Size Bathtub	A	A	I	A	A	I
Microwave	I	A	I	A	I	A
Small Refrigerator	A	I	I	I	A	A
Kitchenette	A	A	A	I	A	A
Appliance Rental Service	I	A	I	I	I	A
VCR	A	A	I	Q	I	A
DVD Player	A	A	I	A	A	A
Carpet	A	A	A	A	A	A
Tile	I	I	I	I	I	I
Enforced Quiet Areas	I	I	I	O	I	M
Vacuum Cleaner Rental Service	M	I	I	I	I	I
Shared Common Vacuum Cleaner	A	I	A	A	A	A
Accessible Roof	A	A	A	A	A	I
Security Guard	I	M	O	M	M	M
Laundry Facility by Floor	O	A	O	O	O	A
Iron and Ironing Board	I	I	I	I	I	I
Optional Laundry Service	A	A	A	A	A	A
Optional Maid Service	A	A	A	A	A	A
Concierge	A	I	A	I	I	A
Reserved Convenient Parking Place	A	A	A	A	A	A
Competitive Admissions (vs. Conventional Assignment)	I	I	I	I	I	I
Admission Based on GPA	R	I	R	R	I	R
Admissions for Business Students Only	R	I	A	R	I	A
Admissions for Junior Level and Up Only	R	I	A	I	I	R
Segregate Residents by Class Level	I	R	I	I	I	O
Armoire	A	A	A	A	A	A
Coffee Table	I	I	I	I	I	I
High Quality Linens	A	A	A	I	I	I
Option to Rent by Semester	A	I	O	I	I	O

Note: *One-Way (O):* User satisfaction is proportional to the performance of the feature; the less performance, the less user satisfaction; and the more performance, the more user satisfaction.

Must-Be (M): User satisfaction is not proportional to the performance of the feature; the less performance, the less user satisfaction; but high performance creates feelings of indifference to the feature.

Attractive (A): User satisfaction is not proportional to the performance of the feature; low levels of performance create feelings of indifference to the feature, but high levels of performance create feelings of delight to the feature.

Indifferent (I): User does not care about the feature.

Questionable (Q): User's response does not make sense (e.g., delighted if feature is present and delighted if feature is absent).

Reverse (R): User offers responses opposite of the expected responses (e.g., "do not like it" if feature is present and "delighted" if feature is absent).

Table 1.16 QFD Table of Feature Used to Respond to Market Segments

Customer Requirements	Single-Occupancy Rooms	Individual Bathrooms	Queen-Size Bed	Broadband Internet	Television Unit	...	Class-Level Segregation	Armoire	Option to Rent by Semester	Importance
									Dormitory Features	
Single-Occupancy Rooms	9	9	0	0	0	...	0	1	3	4.29
Individual Bathrooms	9	9	0	0	0	...	0	0	1	4.60
Queen-Size Bed	3	0	9	0	0	...	0	0	0	4.45
Broadband Internet	0	0	0	9	1	...	0	0	0	4.48
Television Unit	0	0	0	1	9	...	0	3	0	4.44
Telephone Unit	0	0	0	3	0	...	0	0	0	4.00
Cordless Telephone Unit	0	0	0	0	0	...	0	0	0	3.96
Additional Phone Services	0	0	0	1	0	...	0	0	0	4.39
PC Rental Service	0	0	0	1	0	...	0	0	0	3.43
Shared Common Printer	0	0	0	0	0	...	0	0	0	4.16
Large Corner Desk	3	0	0	0	0	...	0	0	0	4.32
Executive Desk Chair	1	0	0	0	0	...	0	0	0	4.36
Additional Desk Chairs	1	0	0	0	0	...	0	3	0	3.82
Climate Control by Room	0	0	0	0	0	...	0	0	0	4.34
Full-Size Bathtub	3	9	0	0	0	...	0	0	0	3.99
...	...	...	...	...	...	...	...	...	...	...
Accessible Roof	0	0	0	0	0	...	1	0	0	4.20
Security Guard	3	1	0	0	1	...	0	0	0	3.96
Laundry Facility by Floor	0	0	0	0	0	...	1	0	0	4.34
Optional Laundry Service	0	0	0	0	0	...	0	0	3	4.07
Optional Maid Service	1	1	0	0	0	...	0	0	3	3.94
Concierge	0	0	0	0	0	...	1	1	3	3.90
Reserved Convenient Parking	0	0	0	0	0	...	1	0	0	4.57
Business Student Admission Only	0	0	0	0	0	...	1	3	1	3.47
Class-Level Segregation	1	0	0	0	0	...	9	0	0	3.22
Armoire	3	0	0	0	3	...	0	9	0	4.45
Option to Rent by Semester	1	0	0	0	0	...	0	0	9	4.25
Unnormalized Weights	173.36	123.72	40.01	80.95	65.21	...	59.83	99.81	94.92	2684.77
Normalized Weights	6.46%	4.61%	1.49%	3.02%	2.43%	...	2.23%	3.72%	3.54%	100.00%

Note: *Importance* is the average response to a survey that asks respondents to rank the importance of each customer requirement (rows in Table 1.16) on a 1 (low importance) to 5 (high importance) scale.

Cell values at the intersection of the rows (Customer Requirements) and columns (Dormitory Features) are interpreted as follows: 0 = no relationship between the customer requirement and the dormitory feature, 1 = weak relationship between the customer requirement and the dormitory feature, 3 = moderate relationship between the customer requirement and the dormitory feature, and 9 = strong relationship between the customer requirement and the dormitory feature.

Un-normalized weights are the sum of the products of the cell values and the importance rankings for a given dormitory feature (column).

Normalized weights are the percentage of the sum of all of the normalized weights for each dormitory feature.

Note that the five designs do not consider common area designs, just the rooms themselves. However, all designs will share the same common area design within the building.

The five designs are graded on six criteria determined by project team members through brainstorming, with Eaton Hall serving as a baseline. The six criteria are:

1. *Willingness of customer to pay more:* luxuries come at a price that must be evaluated with respect to customer price sensitivity. This information was determined by the survey.
2. *Low repair frequency:* a general comparison to the baseline that answers the question: Will this design increase the frequency of needed repairs over that of the baseline?
3. *Ease of repair:* a comparison to the baseline that answers the question: Will this design introduce CTQs (features) that will unduly burden employees in repair and maintenance work?
4. *Replacement frequency:* does the design introduce many CTQs (features) that need yearly replacement?
5. *Easy to clean and maintain:* do any of the introduced CTQs (features) require an inordinate amount of maintenance and cleaning? (As an example of this criterion, fish tanks would score a low grade on this criterion as they require significant upkeep, whereas plastic plants would score high as they only require an occasional dusting.)
6. *Low cost/benefit ratio:* considers the cost of the design and tries to match the soft benefit of appreciation of current university students and the value as a selling point to future students.

The results led to the realization that the "Graduate Preferences" concept is the best concept, with "Undergraduate Preferences" and "Luxury Suite" concepts being possible substitutes.

A Risk Analysis revealed seven potentially serious hazards with the "Graduate Preferences" design:

1. Single-occupancy rooms — potential lack of help in disabling circumstances
2. Kitchenette — potential fire
3. Microwave — potential fire
4. Appliance rental service — potential fire
5. Individual bathrooms — potential lack of help in disabling circumstances
6. Full-size bathtub — potential lack of help in disabling circumstances
7. Accessible roof — potential falls

Finally, a model of the "Graduate Preferences" design was created with Broderbund's 3D Home Architect 4.0 and is depicted in Figure 1.37.

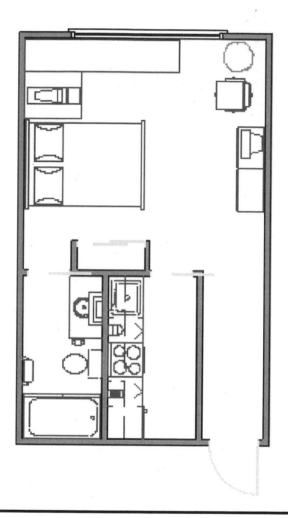

Figure 1.37   Room layout.

Design Phase. The Design Phase of a Design for Lean Six Sigma project has three steps: (1) constructing a detailed design of the "best" design from the Analyze Phase; (2) developing and estimating the capabilities of the specific features (e.g., size and brand of a refrigerator), called critical-to-process (CTPs) elements, in the design; and (3) preparing a verification plan to enable a smooth transition among all affected departments.

Table 1.17 shows the features of the final design for the "Graduate Preferences."

Finally, a residential floor design was developed, given the constraints placed by the dimensions of the plot of land, and the integration of common areas and other required items into the design, such as stairs, elevators, and trash disposal.

Table 1.17 Final Design Features

Feature or Service
Single-Occupancy Rooms
Individual Bathrooms
Queen-Size Bed
Broadband Internet
Television Unit
Telephone Unit
Cordless Telephone Unit
Additional Phone Services
PC Rental Service
Shared Common Printer
Large Corner Desk
Executive Desk Chair
Additional Desk Chairs
Climate Control by Room
Full-Size Bathtub
Microwave
Small Refrigerator
Kitchenette
Appliance Rental Service
VCR
DVD Player
Carpet
Enforced Quiet Areas
Shared Common Vacuum Cleaner
Accessible Roof
Security Guard
Laundry Facility by Floor
Optional Laundry Service
Optional Maid Service
Concierge
Reserved Convenient Parking Place
Admissions for Business Students Only
Segregate Residents by Class Level
Armoire
Option to Rent by Semester

Verify/Validate Phase. The intent of the Verify/Validate Phase is to facilitate buy-in of process owners, to design a control and transition plan, and to conclude the DMADV project.

In the dormitory example, the process owners and all stakeholders were kept intimately involved in the project. A summarized checklist of the findings of this project was developed and should serve as a guide for the engineers and architects who will further develop the project. All bids must include historical process capabilities of the bidding parties. Additionally, a preventive maintenance system per manufacturer recommendations must be implemented after construction. Occupancy indicator control charts must also be implemented.

The final part of the Verify Phase is to maintain communication between the champion and the process owner. These lines of communication will alleviate any confusion or other unforeseen problems that will inevitably develop. It will ensure that the conceptual design is not compromised by outside forces and neglect.

1.2.2.9 Principle 9

Finally, recall that Principle 9 states that planning requires stability. Another example of this principle can be seen in selecting one of two suppliers for purchasing a given item. Both suppliers offer exactly the same product at the same price. Supplier A has a predictable delivery process with an average delivery time of 10 days. Supplier B has a predictable delivery process with an average delivery time of 12 days. At a superficial level, forecasting, planning, and budgeting would seem better using Supplier A because of the lower average delivery time (average = 10 days versus 12 days). However, Supplier B turns out to be the better supplier for forecasting, planning, and budgeting because it has dramatically less variability in its delivery times, although the mean is 20 percent higher (mean = 12 days). That is, Supplier A makes 99.73 percent of its deliveries between 1 and 19 days (see left-hand side of Figure 1.38), while Supplier B makes 99.73 percent of its deliveries between 9 and 15 days (see right-hand side of Figure 1.38). As one can see, Supplier B is the more reliable supplier, even given the higher average time to delivery of goods.

1.2.3 More on Common and Special Causes (Improve the Process to Eliminate Daily Crises)

Dr. W. Edwards Deming stated that, "If anyone adjusts a stable process (one exhibiting only common causes of variation) to try to compensate for a result that is undesirable, or for a result that is extra good, the output that follows will be worse than if he had left the process alone" (see Deming, 1994). The basic problem is treating common causes of variation like special causes of variation, and inappropriately adjusting the process. This is called "over-control of the process, or tampering".

If management tampers with a process without knowledge of how to improve the process through statistical thinking, it will increase the process's variation and

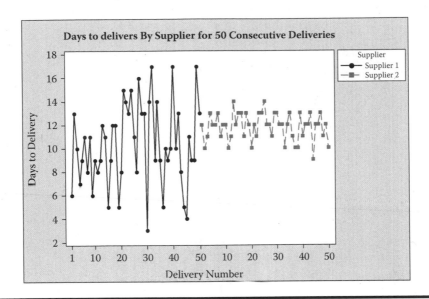

Figure 1.38   Days to deliver goods by supplier for 50 consecutive deliveries for each supplier.

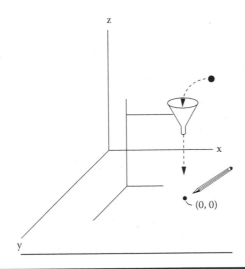

Figure 1.39   Funnel experiment equipment.

reduce its ability to manage that process. Deming (1994) pointed out that "[a] common example is to take action on the basis of a defective item, or on complaint of a customer. The result of his efforts to improve future output (only doing his best) will be to double the variance of the output, or even cause the system to explode.

What is required for improvement is a fundamental healthy change in the system, not tampering."

Loss to an organization results from over-control of its processes, which include safety, training, hiring, supervision, union-management relations, policy formation, production, maintenance, shipping, purchasing, administration, and customer relations, to name a few processes. This loss can be demonstrated by an experiment utilizing a funnel. We will describe the apparatus and procedure for conducting the experiment and then demonstrate its relationship to management's pursuit of continual reduction of variation.

1.2.3.1 The Funnel Experiment

To conduct the experiment, shown in Figure 1.39, we need (1) a funnel, (2) a marble that will fall through the funnel, (3) a flat surface (e.g., a table top) marked with x and y grids such as graph paper, (4) a pencil, and (5) a holder for the funnel.

The experiment involves five steps:

1. Designate a point on the table top (flat surface) as a target and consider this target to be the point of origin in a two-dimensional space, where x and y represent the axes of the surface; hence, at the target (x,y) = (0,0).
2. Drop a marble through the funnel.
3. Mark the spot where the marble comes to rest on the table top (marked as graph paper) with a pencil.
4. Drop the marble through the funnel again and mark the spot where the marble comes to rest on the surface.
5. Repeat Step 4 through 50 drops.

A rule for adjusting the funnel's position in relation to the target is needed to perform Steps 4 and 5. There are four possible rules, and the second rule can be handled in two different ways.

1.2.3.1.1 Rule 1

Set the funnel over the target as best you can at (x = 0, y = 0) and leave the funnel fixed through all 50 drops. This rule will produce a stable pattern of points on the table top; this pattern will approximate a circle, as shown in Figure 1.40. Further, as we will see, the size of the diameters of all circles produced by repeated experimentation using this rule (Rule 1) will be smaller than the size of the diameters resulting from any other rule (that is, Rules 2, 3, or 4) used in Steps 4 and 5 of the experiment.

Management's use of Rule 1 demonstrates an understanding of the distinction between special and common variation, and the different types of managerial action required for each type of variation. Rule 1 implies that the process is being managed by people who know how to reduce variation. *Rule 1 demonstrates an*

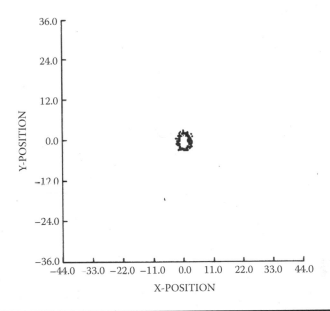

Figure 1.40   Rule 1.

understanding that the position of the marble drops is due only to common causes of variation, and any special action (moving the funnel holder over the floor, that is, the x-y plane) *will only increase the size of the diameter of the circle made by the drops of the marble.* However, moving the funnel up or down is a process improvement. This is discussed at the end of this section.

1.2.3.1.2 Rule 2

The funnel is set over the target at (x = 0,y = 0) prior to the initial drop. Let (x_k,y_k) represent the point where the kth marble dropped through the funnel comes to rest on the surface. Rule 2 states that the funnel should be moved the distance $(-x_k,-y_k)$ from its last resting point — that is, move the funnel in the opposite direction from its current position a distance equal to the distance the marble is from the target. In essence, this is an adjustment rule with a memory of the last resting point. This rule will produce a stable pattern of resting points on the surface, which will approximate a circle. However, the variance of the diameters of all circles produced by repeated experimentation using Rule 2 will have double the diameter of the circular pattern produced using Rule 1, as Figure 1.41 shows.

In terms of its application to management actions, Rule 2 implies that the process is being tampered with by people with inadequate knowledge of how to manage the process to reduce its variation. It implies acting on common variation as if it were special variation. Rule 2 is commonly used as a method of "attempting" to make things better in a process. Here are two examples:

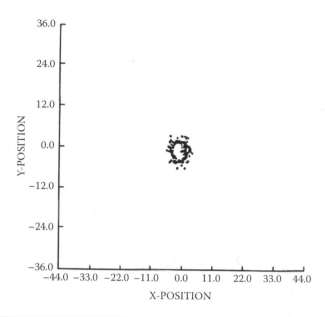

Figure 1.41   Rule 2.

1. *Operator adjustment.* Operator adjustment to compensate for a unit of output's not being on target is an example of Rule 2, assuming adjustments to the process are made from the last process measurement; (see Deming, 1994, pp. 359–360). For example, 3.0 pounds of chemical are to be spread over each 100 square yards of paper in a paper mill. A measuring device continuously monitors the amount of chemical. If the amount of chemical per 100 square yards drops to 2.7 pounds, then the operator increases the amount of chemical to 3.3 pounds to compensate for the 0.3-pound downward drift. If the amount of chemical per 100 square yards jumps to 3.5 pounds, then the operator decreases the amount of chemical from 3.3 pounds to 2.8 pounds to compensate for the 0.5-pound upward drift. And so on.

2. *Automatic process control.* The automatic adjustment of a process to hold output within specified tolerance limits is an example of Rule 2, assuming adjustments to the process are made from the last process measurement. This type of process adjustment procedure is frequently called "rule-based process control (RPC)." RPC is widely used in industry.

1.2.3.1.3 Rule 2a

A variant on Rule 2 is often employed in industry. Rule 2a states if (x_k, y_k) is within a circle centered at $(0,0)$ with diameter d_{spec}, do not adjust the funnel; see Figure 1.42. But if (x_k, y_k) is outside the circle centered at $(0,0)$ with diameter d_{spec}, use the

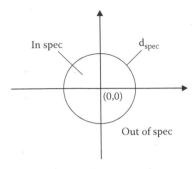

Figure 1.42   Rule 2a.

adjustment rule specified in Rule 2. Rule 2a creates a "dead-band" in which no process adjustment takes place (inside the circle); see Figure 1.42. Rule 2a, with any size dead-band, ultimately yields the same result of doubling the variation of the process as does Rule 2 when compared with Rule 1.

An example of Rule 2a can be seen in variance analysis in cost accounting. One method of monitoring performance in an organization is the use of efficiency and spending variances for the areas of direct labor, direct materials, and overhead. Traditionally, manufacturers in the United States have relied on variance analysis to evaluate performance. If a particular variance is favorable, it is assumed to indicate that acceptable work is being done. If a particular variance is unfavorable, the converse is assumed to be the case.

Variance analysis may cause employees to react inappropriately to accounting variances. That is, variance analysis may force employees to react to variances as if they are due to special causes as opposed to common causes. In the long run, variance analysis doubles the variation of stable processes being managed in accordance with cost accounting principles.

Table 1.18 shows a variance analysis for December 2006. A variance analysis calls for an investigation of any line item that is more than 10 percent different from budget. As you can see, the actual labor overtime expense was $115,000, while the budget for labor overtime was $100,000. This represents a 15-percent overage for the month. Traditional cost accounting would call for an investigation of the reasons for the 15-percent overage in labor overtime. Additionally, you can see that the actual materials expense for December 2006 was $380,000, while the budget for materials was $400,000. This represents a 5-percent underage for the month. In this case, traditional cost accounting would not call for an investigation of the reasons for the 5-percent underage in materials.

Lean Six Sigma management has a completely different approach to explain the variation of each line item from time period to time period (e.g., month to month). For example, labor overtime expense data for January 2005 through December 2006 is shown in Table 1.19.

Table 1.18   Variance Analysis for December 2006

Line Item	Actual Overtime Expense	Budget	Variance
Labor overtime	$115,000	$100,000	($15,000)
Materials	$380,000	$400,000	$20,000

Table 1.19   Data Display

Month	Year	Overtime	Budget	Variance
January	2005	99,385	100,000	−615
February	2005	94,021	100,000	−5,979
March	2005	114,478	100,000	14,478
April	2005	97,663	100,000	−2,337
May	2005	96,274	100,000	−3,726
June	2005	82,417	100,000	−17,583
July	2005	107,138	100,000	7,138
August	2005	82,119	100,000	−17,881
September	2005	109,252	100,000	9,252
October	2005	105,774	100,000	5,774
November	2005	119,033	100,000	19,033
December	2005	105,136	100,000	5,136
January	2006	85,502	100,000	−14,498
February	2006	98,144	100,000	−1,856
March	2006	116,940	100,000	16,940
April	2006	96,964	100,000	−3,036
May	2006	77,610	100,000	−22,390
June	2006	97,244	100,000	−2,756
July	2006	85,247	100,000	−14,753
August	2006	118,253	100,000	18,253
September	2006	120,030	100,000	20,030
October	2006	88,720	100,000	−11,280
November	2006	97,918	100,000	−2,082
December	2006	115,000	100,000	15,000

In Lean Six Sigma management, we create a control chart (Figure 1.43) of the actual labor overtime expense from the data in Table 1.19. The top panel of Figure 1.43 shows that labor overtime expense is a predictable process with a mean of $100,428.00 per month. Further, 99.73 percent of the monthly labor overtime expenses will fall between $144,345.00 and $56,510.00.

As you can see, the overtime expense process naturally varies by more than 10 percent; see Table 1.20. If you look at the variances for January 2005 through December 2006, one sees that 50 percent (12 of 24 in boldface type) of the variances are greater than 10 percent of the budget (i.e., $100,000).

In traditional cost accounting, all 12 of these variances would have to be investigated for special circumstances; and if special circumstances were identified, the process would be inappropriately changed. This is called "tampering with the process, or over-control of the process." It can be proven mathematically that this type of tampering doubles the variation in the budgeting process, making it even less predictable and more problematic (see Gitlow, Kellogg, and Kang, 1992–3).

1.2.3.1.4 Rule 3

The funnel is set over the target at (0,0) prior to the initial drop. Let (x_k,y_k) represent the point where the kth marble dropped through the funnel comes to rest on the surface. Rule 3 states that the funnel should be moved a distance $(-x_k,-y_k)$ from the target (0,0), that is, move the funnel in the opposite direction from the target a distance equal to the distance the marble is from the target. In essence, this is an adjustment rule with no memory of the last resting point of the marble; all corrections are made from the target. This rule will produce an unstable, explosive pattern of resting points on the surface; as k increases, the pattern will move farther and farther away from the target in some symmetrical pattern, such as the bow-tie-shaped pattern in Figure 1.44.

Rule 3 (like Rule 2) is commonly used as a method of "attempting" to improve the process. Rule 3 implies that the process is being tampered with by people with inadequate knowledge of how to manage the process to reduce its variation. It implies acting on common variation as if it were special variation. Here are four examples of Rule 3.

1. *Operator adjustment.* Operator adjustment to compensate for a unit of output's not being on target, or nominal, is an example of Rule 3, assuming adjustments to the process are made from the target and not the last process measurement. Returning to the paper mill example, 3.0 pounds of chemical are to be spread over each 100 square yards of paper in a paper mill. A measuring device continuously monitors the amount of chemical. If the amount of chemical per 100 square yards drops to 2.7 pounds, then the operator increases the amount of chemical from the target of 3.0 pounds to 3.3 pounds to compensate for the 0.3-pound downward drift. If the amount of chemical per 100 square yards

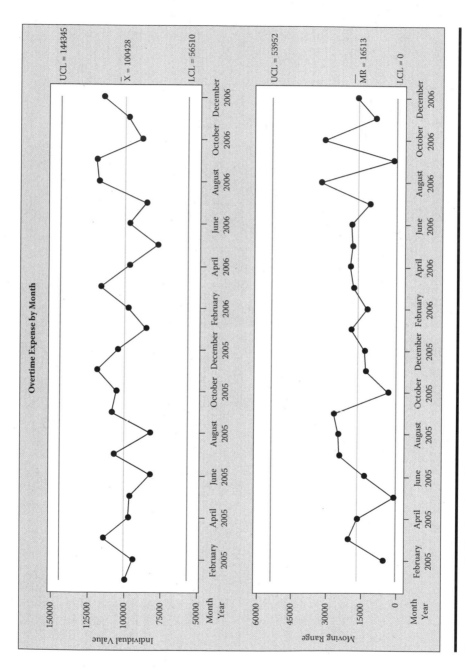

Figure 1.43 Individual and moving range chart of overtime expense per month.

Table 1.20 Proportion Over or Under Budget

Month	Year	Overtime	Budget	Variance	(O-B)/B
January	2005	99,385	100,000	−615	−0.00615
February	2005	94,021	100,000	−5,979	−0.05979
March	2005	114,478	100,000	14,478	**0.14478**
April	2005	97,663	100,000	−2,337	−0.02337
May	2005	96,274	100,000	−3,726	−0.03726
June	2005	82,417	100,000	−17,583	**−0.17583**
July	2005	107,138	100,000	7,138	0.07138
August	2005	82,119	100,000	−17,881	**−0.17881**
September	2005	109,252	100,000	9,252	0.09252
October	2005	10,5774	100,000	5,774	0.05774
November	2005	119,033	100,000	19,033	**0.19033**
December	2005	105,136	100,000	5,136	0.05136
January	2006	85,502	100,000	−14,498	**−0.14498**
February	2006	98,144	100,000	−1,856	−0.01856
March	2006	116,940	100,000	16,940	**0.16940**
April	2006	96,964	100,000	−3,036	−0.03036
May	2006	77,610	100,000	−22,390	**−0.22390**
June	2006	97,244	100,000	−2,756	−0.02756
July	2006	85,247	100,000	−14,753	**−0.14753**
August	2006	118,253	100,000	18,253	**0.18253**
September	2006	120,030	100,000	20,030	**0.20030**
October	2006	88,720	100,000	−11,280	**−0.11280**
November	2006	97,918	100,000	−2,082	−0.02082
December	2006	115,000	100,000	15,000	**0.15000**

Note: (O-B)/B = (Overtime-Budget)/Budget = Proportion over or under budget.

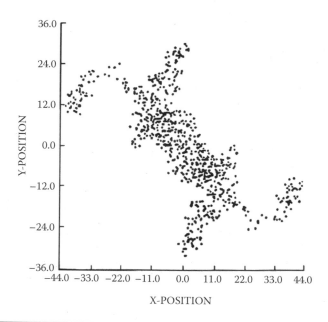

Figure 1.44   Rule 3.

jumps to 3.5 pounds, then the operator decreases the amount of chemical from 3.0 pounds to 2.5 pounds to compensate for the 0.5-pound upward drift. The adjustment is made from the target! And so on.

2. *Automatic process control.* The automatic adjustment of a process to hold output within specified tolerance limits is an example of Rule 3, assuming adjustments to the process are made from the target and not the last process measurement.

3. *Setting the current period's goal based on last period's overage or underage.* A sales quota policy stating that if you are short of this month's goal by $25,000, then you must increase next month's goal by $25,000 is an example of Rule 3.

4. *Making up the previous period's shortage during the current period.* A production policy that requires production personnel to make up any shortages from last month's production run in this month's production run is an example of Rule 3.

1.2.3.1.5 Rule 4

The funnel is set over the target at (0,0) prior to the initial drop. Let (x_k, y_k) represent the point where the kth marble dropped through the funnel comes to rest on the surface. Rule 4 states that the funnel should be moved to the resting point, (x_k, y_k); that is, move the funnel to the resting point of the most recently dropped marble. This is a phenomenally stupid rule for hitting the target. In essence, this is an adjustment rule with no memory of either the last resting point of the marble

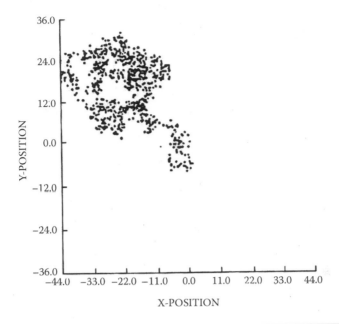

Figure 1.45 Rule 4.

or the position of the target at (0,0). This rule will produce an unstable, explosive pattern of resting points on the surface as k increases without bound, and it will eventually move farther and farther away from the target at (0,0) in one direction, as shown in Figure 1.45.

Rule 4 is commonly used as a method of "attempting" to make things better in a process. Rule 4 implies that the process is being tampered with by people with inadequate knowledge of how to manage the process to reduce its variation. It implies acting on common variation as if it were special variation. Here are nine examples of Rule 4.

- *The telephone game.* The telephone game that children play is an example of Rule 4. In the game, the first child whispers something to the second, the second whispers the same thing to the third child, and so on, until the last child announces what he has just heard. The message gets continually more confusing, and after a time the current message bears no resemblance to the original message.
- *The grapevine.* People who take action in their personal and professional lives based on information from the "grapevine" or "rumor mill" are using Rule 4 as a basis for action. Their next action is a function of only the most recent past action.
- *On-the-job training.* This is a horrific example of Rule 4 where people on a job train a new worker. This worker is then ready after a while to train a new

worker. The methods taught deteriorate without bound. Possible solutions to this problem are to formalize training with a DVD presentation or to utilize a master in the subject matter to do the training, to get a consistent and desired message to the trainees.

- *Make it like the last one.* Using the last unit of output as the standard for the next unit of output will eventually produce material bearing no resemblance to the original piece — an example of Rule 4. A possible solution to this problem is to use a master piece as a point of comparison.
- *Budgeting.* Setting the next period's budget as a percentage of the last period's budget is an example of Rule 4.
- *Engineering changes.* Engineering changes to a product or process based on the latest version of a design without regard to the original design are made in accordance with Rule 4. Eventually, the current design will bear no resemblance to the original design.
- *Policy surveys.* An executive who changes policy based on results of the latest employee survey, in a stream of employee surveys, is operating under Rule 4. Eventually, the policy will have no bearing on its original intended purpose.
- *Adjusting work standards to reflect current performance.* An organization that adjusts work standards to reflect current conditions is using Rule 4. Work standards should be replaced with control charts that allow management to understand the capability of a process and take action to improve the process by reducing the variation in the process.
- *Collective bargaining.* Union–management negotiations in which successive contracts are a reaction to current conditions is an example of Rule 4.

1.2.3.1.6 Conclusion

The funnel experiment illustrates how a system is improved not by tampering (over-control of common variation), but by reducing common variation. In the experiment, this means reducing the diameter of the circle created under Rule 1 either by moving the funnel closer to the surface or by straightening and lengthening the tube portion of the funnel to reduce the dispersion among the resting points. Note that both methods for improvement are system changes. In terms of an organization, the corresponding reduction in variation also involves system changes. As management is responsible for the system, only management can make the necessary changes to reduce this variation in the system.

1.2.3.2 The Red Bead Experiment

The red bead experiment (see Deming, 1994, pp. 154–171) is another well-known illustration of the negative effects of treating common variation as special variation. It is discussed in this section to further enhance the reader's understanding of common causes and special causes of variation.

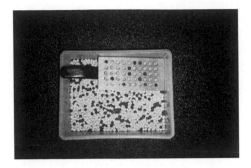

Figure 1.46   Bead box with paddle.

The experiment involves using a paddle to select beads from a box that contains 4000 beads, as shown in Figure 1.46. The box contains 3200 white beads and 800 red beads. This fact is unknown to the participants in the experiment.

In the experiment, a foreman in the Quality Bead Company hires, trains, and supervises: (1) four "willing workers" to produce white beads, (2) two inspectors of the willing workers' output, (3) one chief inspector to inspect the findings of the inspectors, and (4) one recorder of the chief inspector's findings. A willing worker's job consists of using a paddle that has five rows of ten bead-size holes to select 50 beads from the box of beads.

Once the employees of the Quality Bead Company have been hired, the foreman trains them using detailed instructions and highly supervised practice sessions in their appropriate job responsibilities and procedures. The job of the workers is to produce white beads, because red beads are unacceptable to customers. Strict procedures are to be followed. Daily work standards call for the production of 50 beads by each worker (a strict quota system): no more and no less than 50. Management has established a standard that no more than three red beads (6 percent) per worker are permitted on any given day. The beads are mixed by pouring them from one container to another and then back again *before* each worker draws his or her daily workload of 50 beads. After mixing, each worker dips the paddle into the box of beads so that when it is removed, each of the 50 holes contains a bead. Once this is done, the paddle is carried to each of the two inspectors, who independently record the count of red beads. The chief inspector compares their counts and announces the results to the recorder who writes down the number and percentage of red beads next to the name of the worker.

Once all the people know their jobs, "production" then begins. On the first day, the number of red beads produced by the four workers (Alyson, David, Peter, and Sharyn) was 9, 12, 13, and 7, respectively. How should management react to the day's production when the standard says that no more than three red beads per worker should be produced? Should all the workers be reprimanded, or should only David and Peter be given a stern warning that they will be fired if they do not improve?

Production continues for an additional 2 days. Table 1.21 summarizes the results for all three days.

From Table 1.21, we can observe several phenomena. On each day, some of the workers were above the average and some below the average. On day 1, Sharyn did best; on day 2, Peter (who had the worst record on day 1) was best; and on day 3, Alyson was best.

How then can we explain all this variation, especially given all the training provided to employees by the foreman? Figure 1.47 indicates that the worker-to-worker variation in the proportion of red beads over the three days forms a stable and predictable system. That is, there are no differences between the willing workers over

Table 1.21 Number of Red Beads Produced by Worker by Day

Name	Day 1	2	3	All 3 Days
Alyson	9	11	6	26
David	12	12	8	32
Peter	13	6	12	31
Sharyn	7	9	8	24
All 4 workers	41	38	34	113

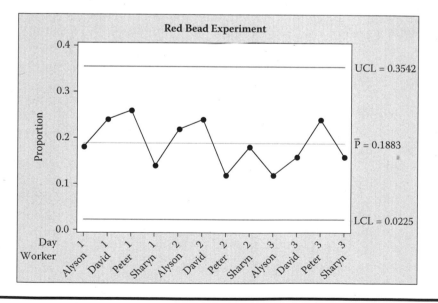

Figure 1.47 Control chart of proportion of red beads by worker by day.

the 3 days other than random noise (common causes of variation). All proportions of red beads randomly bounce around an average proportion of red beads of 0.1883, and lie between the statistical signal limits of 0.3542 and 0.0225*. Granted, the system of production of white beads in the Quality Bead Company is very noisy. If the management is not satisfied with the results, then they must improve the system — and not blame the willing workers by punishing and rewarding them using the production quota (50 beads per day) with its quality standard (no more than three red beads in a workload). One way management could improve the system of production in the Quality Bead Company is to use a different bead supplier that delivers beads with a lower proportion of red beads in their shipments. Another method management could use to improve the system of production is to switch from a paddle to a vacuum straw that is only aimed at white beads.

Frequently, it is better to begin process improvement efforts within your own area *before* demanding it of your suppliers. Remember that suppliers can be the process upstream from your process. Putting your own process in order is frequently necessary before you demand it from your suppliers.

Some of the lessons of the red bead experiment include:

1. Common variation is an inherent part of any process.
2. Managers are responsible for the common variation in a system; they set the policies and procedures.
3. Worker bees are not responsible for the problems of the system, that is, common causes of variation. The system primarily determines the performance of workers.
4. Only management can change the system.
5. Some worker bees will always be above the average, and some will always be below the average.
6. If the inspectors disagree with their red bead counts, there may be a problem. If the inspectors agree with their red bead counts, there may be a problem. Inspection is *not* an effective tool for producing quality output. A better method is improving the process to get better output.

1.2.3.3 Feedback Loops

An important aspect of any process is a feedback loop. A feedback loop relates information about outputs from any stage or stages back to another stage or stages so that an analysis of the process can be made. Figure 1.48 depicts the feedback loop in relation to a basic process. A major purpose of Lean Six Sigma management is to provide the information (flowing through a feedback loop) needed to take action with respect to a process. A feedback loop is used to collect data on the metrics (key indicators) needed to turn the PDSA cycle or use the DMAIC model.

---

* $p = 0.1883$; $UCL = p + 3\sqrt{[p(1 - p)/n]} = 0.1883 + 3\sqrt{[0.1883(1 - 0.1883)/50]} = 0.3542$; and $LCL = p - 3\sqrt{[p(1-p)/n]} = 0.1883 - 3\sqrt{[0.1883(1 - 0.1883)/50]} = 0.0225$.

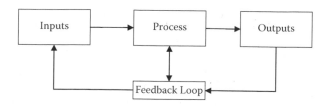

Figure 1.48   Feedback loop.

There are three feedback loop situations: (1) no feedback loop, (2) special cause only feedback loop, and (3) special and common cause feedback loop. A *no feedback loop* process that does not have a feedback loop is probably doomed to deterioration and decay (called "entropy") due to the inability of its stakeholders to rejuvenate and improve it based on data (metrics) from its outputs. An example of a process without a feedback loop is a relationship between two people (manager and subordinate, husband and wife, or buyer and seller) that contains no vehicle (feedback loop) to discuss issues and problems with the intention of establishing a better relationship in the future. A *special cause only feedback loop* process will exhibit enormous variation in its output. This was discussed in Section 1.2.3.1 on the Funnel Experiment; see Rules 2, 3, and 4. An example of a process with a special cause only feedback loop can again be seen in a relationship between a boss and a subordinate, but in this case the relationship deteriorates through a cycle of successive overreactions to problems that are perceived as special by both members of the relationship. In fact, the problems are probably repetitive in nature, due to the structure of the relationship itself and common causes of variation. Finally, a *common and special case feedback loop* process in which special causes are resolved, and common causes are removed, will exhibit continuous improvement of its output. For example, relationship problems between a boss and a subordinate can be classified as either special or common; statistical methods can be used to identify special causes and to resolve them, and to remove common causes, thereby improving the relationship in the future.

1.2.4 Four Questions You May Ask about Lean Six Sigma Management

Four questions you may want to ask about "Lean Six Sigma" management are:

1. Will I get more work if I improve my job?
2. Will I get fired if the improvement(s) I make eliminate my job?
3. Will I get release time from my regular job to work on Lean Six Sigma projects?
4. Will I get a share of the financial benefits generated by my Lean Six Sigma project efforts?

These questions are a natural reaction to the transformation defined by pursuing Lean Six Sigma management. Transformation (change) is a difficult, soul-searching activity that has a profound effect on the individual and the organization. It takes courage and strength of character to involve oneself in change. Top management must have a burning desire and personal discipline to transform its organization, and worker bees must have the personal discipline to follow the best-practice methods developed through Lean Six Sigma projects.

Worker bees should realize that lack of commitment by top management for transformation will kill a Lean Six Sigma effort. If transformation promises improvement in all areas of the organization, why do all top managers not embrace it? First, top managers may not be pro Lean Six Sigma because it is not their own creation. Second, they may fear failure to meet the short-term goals established as part of a Management by Objectives (MBO) system. Third, executives are reluctant to change because they have been personally successful; the organization beneath them may be falling apart, but as long as they continue to get raises and positive performance appraisals, they can deny the rampant problems.

Back to the four questions listed above. Each one can be answered from the perspective of a worker bee:

1. The answer to the first question — "Will I get more work if I improve my job?" — has two parts, depending on the nature of your "overtime work." If you do no "overtime work," then you will still be expected to put in a full work week. However, your work will not be as pressured and stressful as it was before the improvement (or improvements) to your job. If you do "overtime work" for extra compensation, then you may see a dramatic reduction in overtime hours. For some workers, this reduction is a welcome change because of more leisure time. For other workers, this reduction is a loss of income. One solution to this loss of income is to expand your skill set to attract higher-paying "overtime work." Higher-paying "overtime work" will likely result in more "joy in work." *If you do uncompensated overtime work, then your life is about to get much better!*

2. The answer to the second question — "Will I get fired if the improvement(s) I make eliminate my job?" — in a true Lean Six Sigma company is an emphatic no. First, if you are an employee who understands Lean Six Sigma and has used it to improve one or more processes, then you are very valuable. A manager would be "nuts" to fire you. In a Lean Six Sigma company, labor reductions due to process improvement are accomplished using planning, patience, and natural attrition (retires, relocates, quits, etc.), *not* firing the people who are making the company more profitable.

3. The answer to the third question — "Will I get release time from my regular job to work on Lean Six Sigma projects?" — is not so clear. Some Lean Six Sigma companies require that project work provides a reduction to your regular work, while others do not. Regardless, if management is serious about

"Lean Six Sigma," then the short-term increase in project work is worth the long-term reduction in workload, pressure, and stress. That is, "the juice is usually worth the squeeze."

4. The answer to the fourth question — "Will I get a share of the financial benefits generated by my Lean Six Sigma project efforts?" — is a function of management's truly adopting the theory underlying Lean Six Sigma management. The theory calls for a dramatically different view of motivation. The current practice of management relies primarily on extrinsic motivators (rewards and punishments) from a Management by Objectives (MBO) system to motivate people. Usually, the financial rewards of project work are *not* shared with the worker bees in a company. On the other hand, Lean Six Sigma management promotes a balance between extrinsic motivators and intrinsic motivators (that is, joy in work). Intrinsic motivators involve worker bees using Lean Six Sigma methods to improve their work and being motivated by the sheer pleasure of the act of work. Extrinsic motivators include pay raises, promotions, and in some cases, profit-sharing. For a more complete discussion of compensation systems in a Lean Six Sigma company, see the next chapter of this book.

Chapter 2

Motivation and Compensation

2.1 Traditional View: Extrinsic Motivators

Extrinsic motivators are techniques used by management to stimulate an employee's efforts toward a particular goal, for example, more profitability or greater customer satisfaction. Traditional management employs several types of extrinsic motivators, depending on the level of an employee in an organization. Management by objectives, enforced through the Performance Appraisal System (PAS), is used to motivate top and middle management. Sales quotas are used to motivate salespeople.

Production quotas are used to motivate supervisors and hourly workers. And finally, piecework standards are also used to motivate workers. Additional forms of extrinsic motivators include, but are not limited to, employee of the month programs, free movie tickets, a free trip to Hawaii for an employee and his or her spouse, promotions and demotions, pay raises and decreases, bonuses, and a pat on the back for a job well done.

Extrinsic motivators can be expensive and short-lived. People rapidly become used to the extrinsic motivator and it loses its effectiveness, and frequently, performance returns to its previous level.

The above facts beg the question: How are you going to manage your people to prevent them from becoming depressed, despondent, and unproductive in economically depressed times? In other words, what happens in economic times when you do not have any resources (extrinsic motivators) to give to your people. You can always give your people a free pat on the back for a job well done. Unfortunately, this type of motivator loses its effectiveness in the absence of financial motivators. They can even become irritating and demotivating. So, back to the question: How are you going to manage your people to prevent them from becoming depressed, despondent, and unproductive in economically depressed times? There is no effective answer in the traditional paradigm of management.

One possible negative result of the exclusive use of extrinsic motivators to stimulate people in economically depressed times is hearing the following expression: "Just shut up and be glad you have your job." This indicates a manager who is at his or her wits' end. The manager may want to give you a financial extrinsic reward but has none to give. In the face of your perceived constant nagging for a raise, bonus, etc., your frustrated manager blurts out: "Just shut up and be glad you have your job."

The cost and short life of an extrinsic motivator can be seen in the following real example. An associate professor was promoted to full professor and received a 30 percent pay raise at the age of 32 years. This was the final promotion in his life. He was *flying* in the stratosphere of extrinsic motivation. About two weeks after the promotion, he dismissed a graduate class about five minutes early. This is a sin, but an extremely small sin in the academic world, but a sin nonetheless. The academic dean responsible for the associate professor's promotion saw the early dismissal, called the professor into his office, and proceeded to "take him to the woodshed." The professor claimed he could see a pool of extrinsic motivation at his feet, at least he assumed it was extrinsic motivation. The point of the story is that the university got two weeks of benefits from a *very* expensive extrinsic motivator.

In summary, extrinsic motivation comes from the desire for reward or the fear of punishment. It may restrict the release of energy from intrinsic motivation by judging, policing, and destroying the individual. Management based solely on extrinsic motivation may crush the spirit of intrinsic motivation in employees; see Deming (1994, p. 109).

2.2 Lean Six Sigma View: Intrinsic and Extrinsic Motivators

2.2.1 Background

People are best inspired by a mix of intrinsic and extrinsic motivation, not solely by extrinsic motivation. Intrinsic motivation comes from the sheer joy of performing an act. It releases human energy that can focus on the improvement and innovation of a system. It is management's responsibility to create an atmosphere that fosters a balance between intrinsic and extrinsic motivators.

Managers cannot give employees intrinsic motivation. However, managers can extrinsically create a work environment that encourages employees to use the PDSA cycle (Plan, Do, Study, and Act cycle) to improve their jobs. As their jobs improve through their own intellectual contributions, they will see increases in their own productivity, increases in their customers' satisfaction, decreases in their levels of stress, decreases in the number of crises they experience per day, and *a decrease in the amount of uncompensated overtime.* As this occurs, employees feel intrinsic motivation and the burst of energy it releases into the bloodstream. This is one of the key pillars of effective Lean Six Sigma management.

An illustration of the power contained in balancing intrinsic and extrinsic motivators can be seen in the following real example. A 50-year-old man was 25 pounds overweight, had high cholesterol and blood pressure, and had severe lower back pain. His physician told him in no uncertain terms that if he did not change his lifestyle, he would have a stroke. Needless to say, this scared him a lot. This type of focused fear can be a powerful extrinsic motivator, and in this case it was. He immediately began to see a nutritionist and exercise on a regular basis. His weight dropped by 25 pounds, his cholesterol and blood pressure were significantly lowered, and his back pain disappeared. His body shape began to look more like a "V" that an "O." His wife told him he was looking good. All these events were significant extrinsic motivators. However, getting healthy and staying healthy are two different issues. As he began to feel and look better, he started to experience intrinsic motivation in his new lifestyle. Now it is ten years later and he still is in good shape. He knows he could not have maintained his current condition solely from extrinsic motivators. His success was sustained by balancing extrinsic and intrinsic motivators.

You may be wondering: What would a performance appraisal system that balances extrinsic and intrinsic motivators look like? Can it really exist? These are fair questions. A Lean Six Sigma based performance appraisal system that balances extrinsic and intrinsic motivators is described below.

2.2.2 Lean Six Sigma and Performance Appraisal

The owner and operator of a chain of retail flower shops decided to structure his company according to Lean Six Sigma principles. A performance appraisal system had to be developed at the time the company was formed. Because the executive team of the chain wanted it to be in keeping with Lean Six Sigma, a cross-functional team composed of the top management of selected departments was formed. The cross-functional team followed a five-step process to construct the Lean Six Sigma performance appraisal system; it is presented below.

Step 1: First, the team states a mission for the proposed performance appraisal system. It is "to develop a performance appraisal system consistent with Lean Six Sigma management principles." This mission is made clear to all employees.

Step 2: Then, team members identify all stakeholders of the performance appraisal process: candidates, new hires, employees, supervisors, and top management.

Step 3: The team constructs an integrated flowchart of a traditional human resource system, with special attention paid to the performance appraisal functions, as shown in the shaded sections in column one of Figure 2.1.

Step 4: Team members identify key measures of the efficiency and effectiveness of the performance appraisal system. The *efficiency* of the performance appraisal process is measured by the percent of performance appraisals completed on time, by supervisor, and overall, by year. The *effectiveness* of the performance appraisal process is measured by:
■ Percent of performance appraisals with written comments concerning improvement of work by appraisal period.
■ List of responses from employees to the question, "Did you know what to do to improve your job performance upon leaving your performance review?" by year.

Step 5: Team members developed modifications to the integrated flowchart shown in Figure 2.1 that balances extrinsic and intrinsic motivators; see Scholtes (1987). Scholtes identified the following functions as the components of a performance appraisal system:
■ Provide feedback to employees on their work.
■ Provide a basis for salary increases and bonuses.
■ Identify candidates for promotion.
■ Provide periodic direction of an employee's work.
■ Provide an opportunity to give recognition, direction, and feedback regarding special projects.
■ Identify needs for training, education, and skill or career development.
■ Provide an equitable, objective, defensible system that satisfies the requirements of the Civil Rights Act and the Equal Opportunity Commission guidelines.
■ Provide a channel for communication.

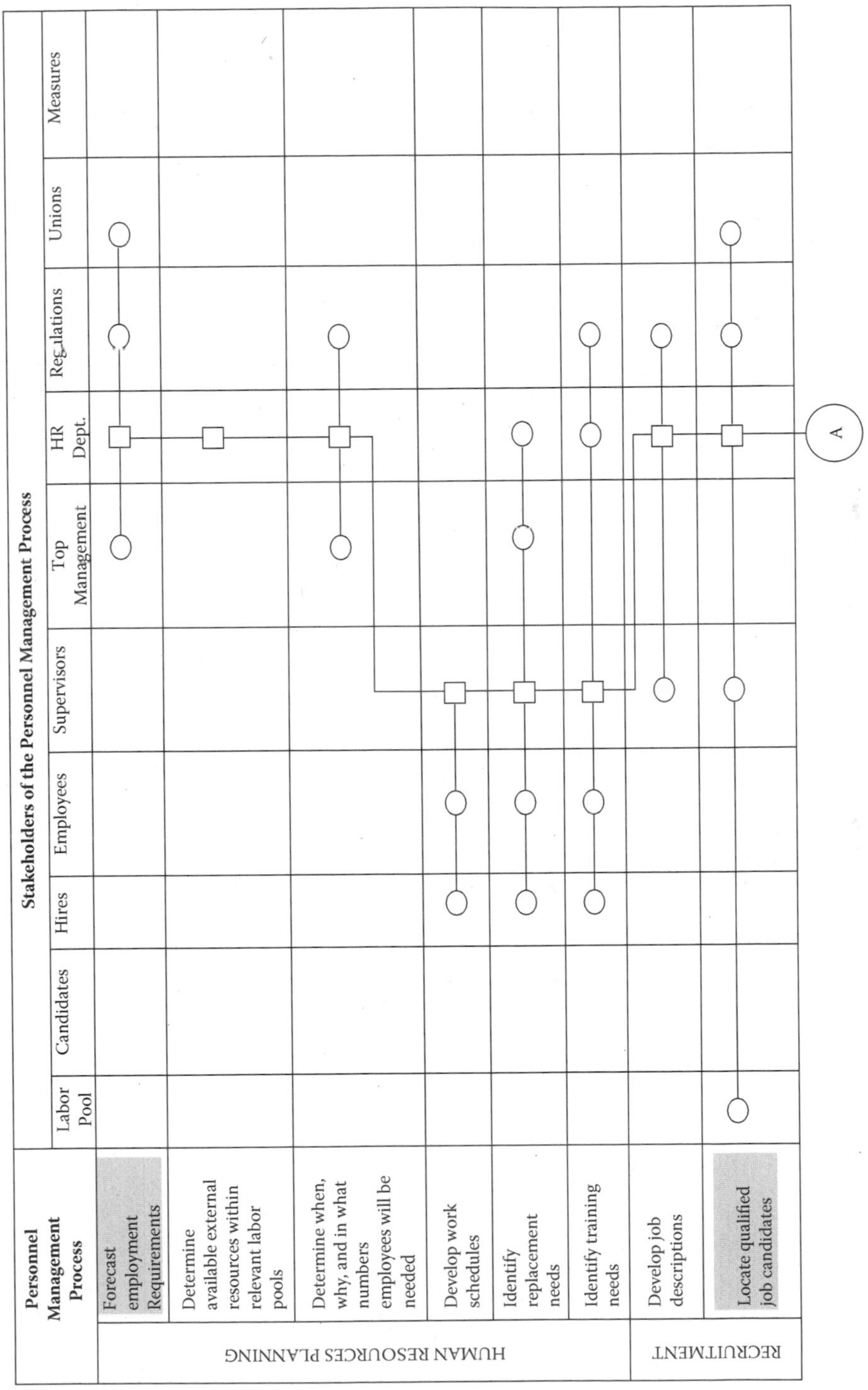

Figure 2.1 Integrated flowchart of the personnel management process.

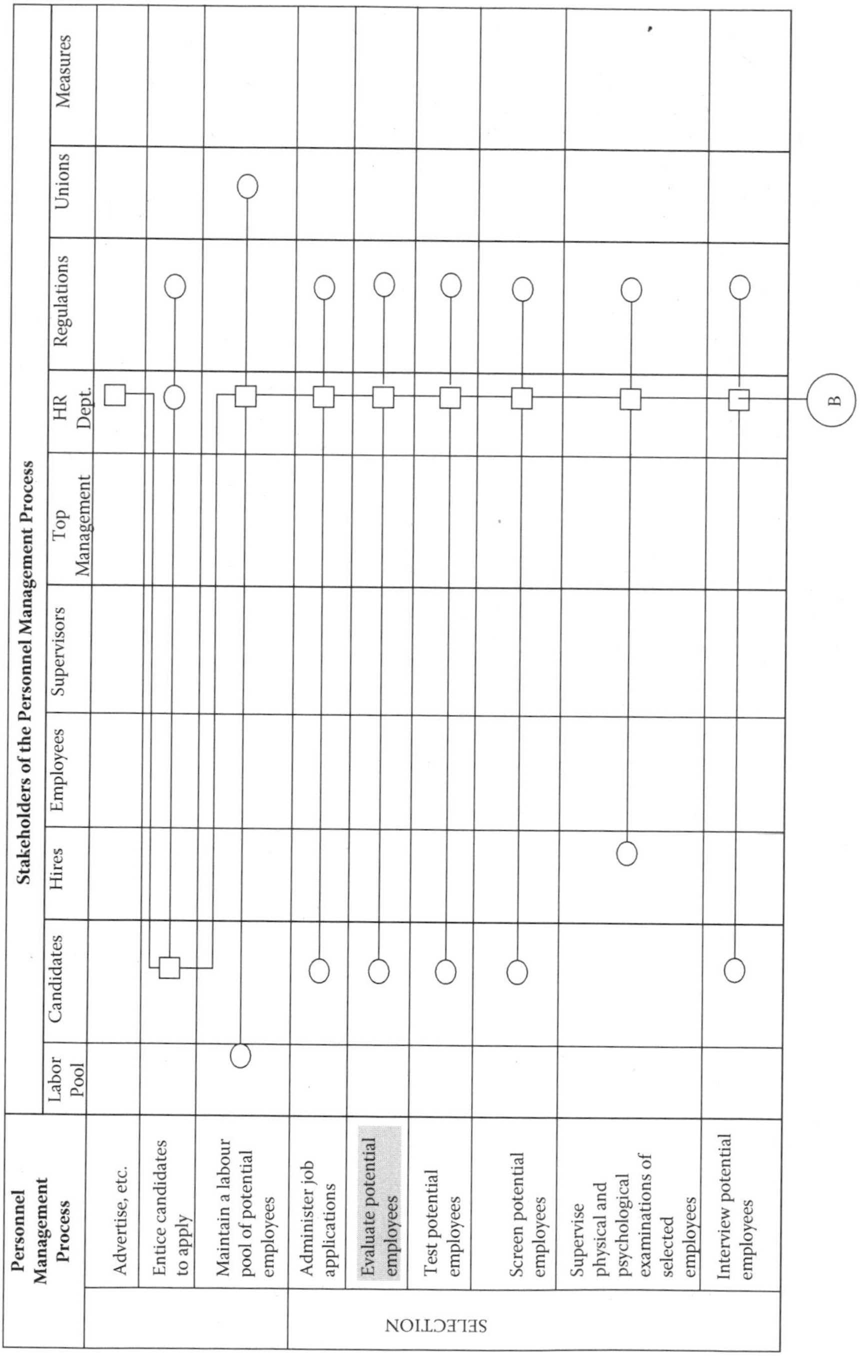

Personnel Management Process	Stakeholders of the Personnel Management Process									
	Labor Pool	Candidates	Hires	Employees	Supervisors	Top Management	HR Dept.	Regulations	Unions	Measures
SELECTION										
Advertise, etc.							□			
Entice candidates to apply		□					○	○		
Maintain a labour pool of potential employees	○								○	
Administer job applications		○					□	○		
Evaluate potential employees		○					□	○		
Test potential employees		○					□	○		
Screen potential employees		○					□	○		
Supervise physical and psychological examinations of selected employees			○				□	○		
Interview potential employees		○					□	○		

(B)

Figure 2.1 (continued)

Personnel Management Process		Stakeholders of the Personnel Management Process									
		Labor Pool	Candidates	Hires	Employees	Supervisors	Top Management	HR Dept.	Regulations	Unions	Measures
	Select finalists		○					□			
	Send finalists to Hiring department		○			○		□			
	Interview potential finalists		○			□					
	Select hiree		○			□	○	○			
	Hire employee			○		○	○	□	○	○	
	File paperwork							□	○		
ORIENTATION	Familiarize employees with company policy			○				□	○		
ORIENTATION	Familiarize employees with safety codes			○				□	○		
ORIENTATION	Familiarize employees with objectives			○		○		□	○		
ORIENTATION	Familiarize employees with work expectations			○		○		□	○		
ORIENTATION	If appropriate, provide technical training in specific work conditions			○		○		□	○		

C

Figure 2.1 (continued)

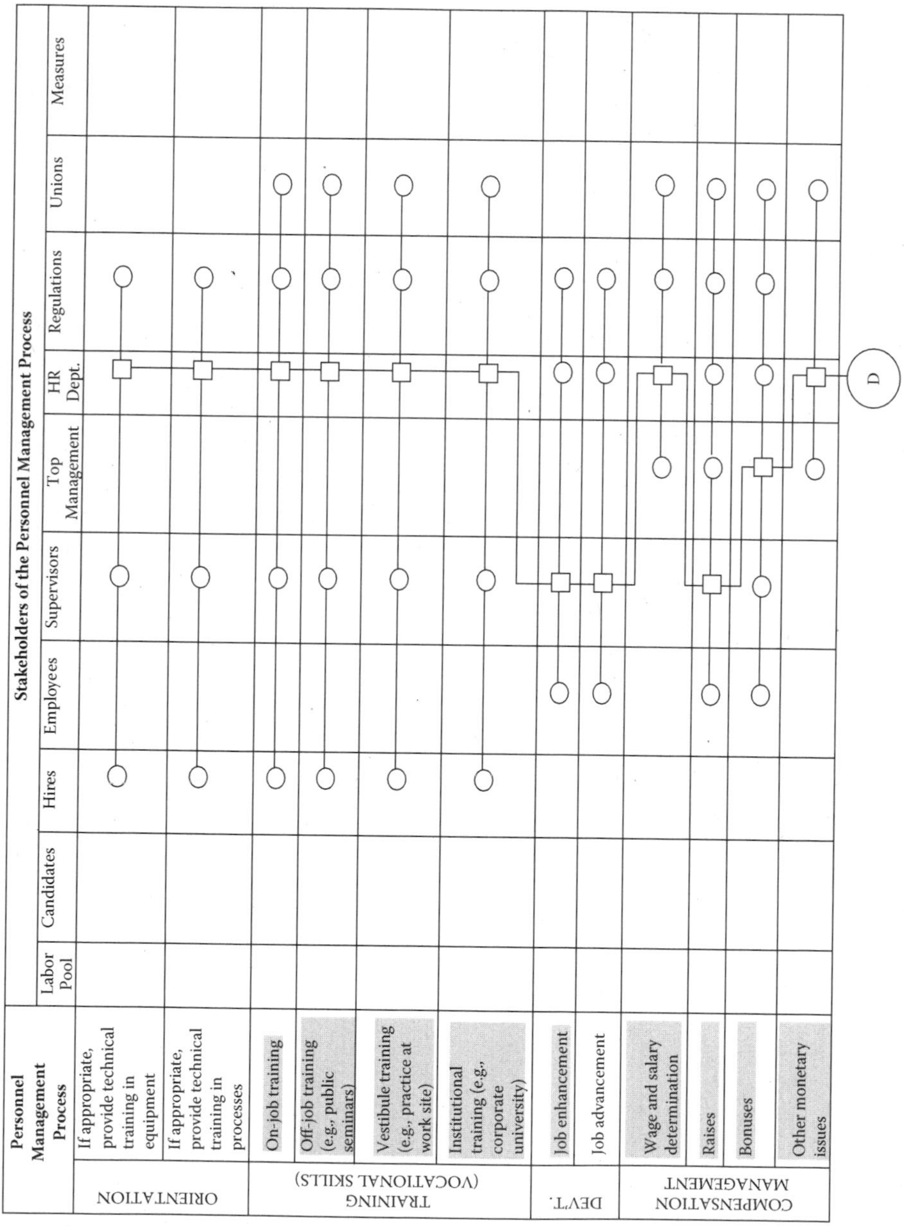

Personnel Management Process		Stakeholders of the Personnel Management Process									
		Labor Pool	Candidates	Hires	Employees	Supervisors	Top Management	HR Dept.	Regulations	Unions	Measures
ORIENTATION	If appropriate, provide technical training in equipment			O		O		□	O		
	If appropriate, provide technical training in processes			O		O		□	O		
TRAINING (VOCATIONAL SKILLS)	On-job training			O		O		□	O	O	
	Off-job training (e.g., public seminars)			O		O		□	O	O	
	Vestibule training (e.g., practice at work site)			O		O		□	O	O	
	Institutional training (e.g., corporate university)			O		O		□	O	O	
DEV'T.	Job enhancement				O	□	O	O	O	O	
	Job advancement				O	□		O	O	O	
COMPENSATION MANAGEMENT	Wage and salary determination					□	□	□	O	O	
	Raises				O		O	O	O	O	
	Bonuses						□	O	O	O	
	Other monetary issues				O		O	□	O	O	

D

Figure 2.1 (continued)

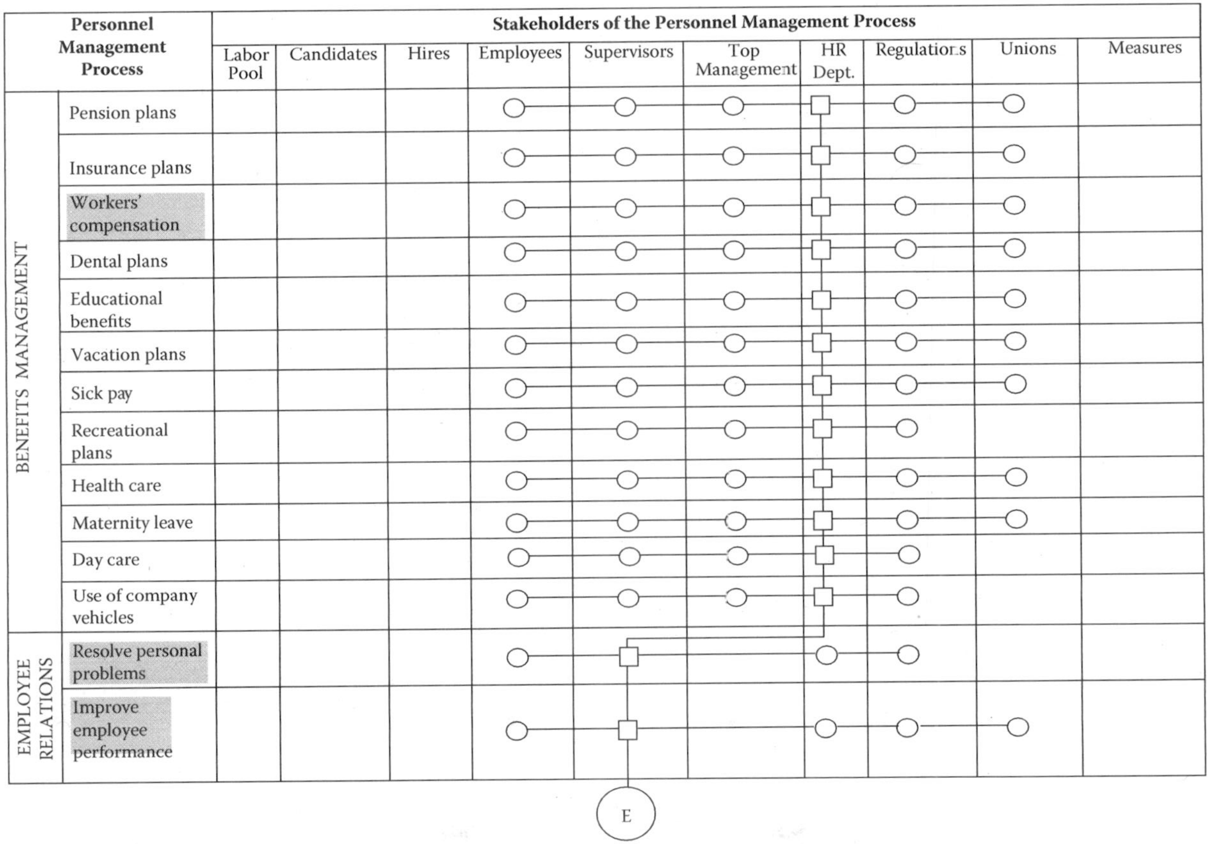

Personnel Management Process	Stakeholders of the Personnel Management Process								
	Labor Pool	Candidates	Hires	Employees	Supervisors	Top Management	HR Dept.	Regulations	Unions	Measures
BENEFITS MANAGEMENT Pension plans				O	O	O	□	O	O	
Insurance plans				O	O	O	□	O	O	
Workers' compensation				O	O	O	□	O	O	
Dental plans				O	O	O	□	O	O	
Educational benefits				O	O	O	□	O	O	
Vacation plans				O	O	O	□	O	O	
Sick pay				O	O	O	□	O		
Recreational plans				O	O	O	□	O	O	
Health care				O	O	O	□	O	O	
Maternity leave				O	O	O	□	O		
Day care				O	O	O	□	O		
Use of company vehicles				O	O	O	□	O		
EMPLOYEE RELATIONS Resolve personal problems				O	□	O	O	O		
Improve employee performance				O	□		O	O	O	

E

Figure 2.1 (continued)

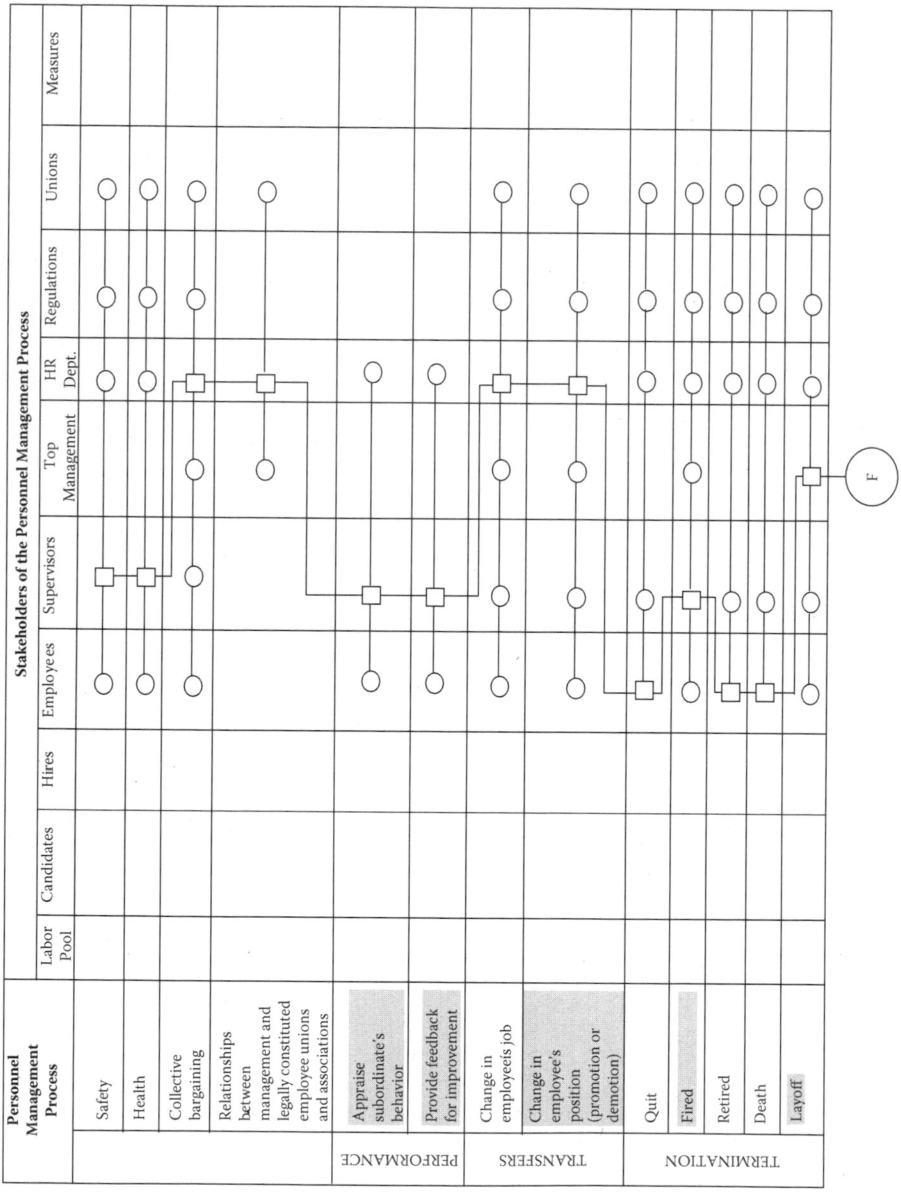

Stakeholders of the Personnel Management Process

Personnel Management Process		Labor Pool	Candidates	Hires	Employees	Supervisors	Top Management	HR Dept.	Regulations	Unions	Measures
PERFORMANCE	Safety				O	O		O	O	O	
	Health				O	□		O	O	O	
	Collective bargaining				O	O	O	□	O	O	
	Relationships between management and legally constituted employee unions and associations						O	□			
	Appraise subordinate's behavior				O	□		O			
	Provide feedback for improvement				O	□		O			
TRANSFERS	Change in employee is job				O	O	O	□		O	
	Change in employee's position (promotion or demotion)				O	O	O	□		O	
TERMINATION	Quit				□	O			O	O	
	Fired				O	□	O	O	O	O	
	Retired				□	□		O	O	O	
	Death				□	O		O	O	O	
	Layoff				O	O	□ (F)	O	O	O	

Figure 2.1 (continued)

2.2.3 The Revised Performance Appraisal System

The *provide feedback for improvement step* in the *Performance Evaluation* section of Figure 2.1 is redefined to be providing employees feedback on work. Feedback can be provided by following the steps listed below:

- Identify the major processes in which the employee is involved.
- Identify the major work group or groups to which the employee belongs.
- Develop a list of major feedback sources for the employee (e.g., key customers, suppliers, and process outputs).
- Develop a method, with objectives and indicators, to obtain feedback from each feedback resource.

This type of feedback is a powerful extrinsic motivator.

The *wage and salary determination, raises, bonuses, and other monetary issues* steps in the *Compensation Management* section and the *workers' compensation* step in the *Benefits Management* section of Figure 2.1 are redefined to be:

- Provide a basis for salary increases and bonuses based on market rate (what it would cost to replace someone on the open market?).
- Accumulate skills (flexibility due to acquired abilities).
- Accumulate responsibility (depth of contribution to a greater number of processes and influence over a larger number of employees).
- Value seniority within an organization and within a job classification.
- Share prosperity (gain-sharing or profit-sharing of the entire organization, not just one segment of the organization).

This type of feedback stimulates both extrinsic and intrinsic motivation. It provides extrinsic motivators in the giving of raises, bonuses, and other monetary rewards. It involves intrinsic motivators in the joy in improving oneself from accumulating additional responsibilities and acquiring more training and education. Compensation is the last part of the Human Resources system to be changed. The above makes sense *only* in an environment of continuous improvement of all processes. If the above changes are made prematurely, then "the lazy will inherit the earth."

The *change in employee's position [promotion or demotion]* step in the *Transfers* section of Figure 2.1 is redefined to be:

- Identify candidates for promotion by providing special assignments that contain elements of the promotion job.
- Utilize an assessment center to observe candidates exercising the skills needed in the promotion job under realistic conditions (if available).

■ Determine the needs and wants of the stakeholders of the promotion job with respect to the characteristics of the person who will assume the promotion job, and identify the person with the best match for the promotion job.

■ Develop an organizational culture in which promotion is not the only vehicle for people to exercise leadership and influence, to get rewards and recognition, or to stretch and challenge themselves in their jobs and careers.

Promotions and demotions are extremely powerful extrinsic motivators.

The *familiarize employees with objectives* and *familiarize employees with work expectations* steps of the *Orientation* section of Figure 2.1 is redefined to be:

■ Provide periodic direction to each employee by communicating the mission, key objectives, and key indicators of the organization.

■ Spend time with each employee to develop, improve, and innovate the processes necessary for each employee to pursue his mission, key objectives, and key indicators (job).

Again, this type of information provides powerful extrinsic motivators. It also can stimulate intrinsic motivation by helping the employee see how he or she fits into the larger organization.

The *job enhancement* step of the *Development (Managerial Skills)* section and the *appraise subordinate's behavior* step of the *Performance Evaluation* section of Figure 2.1 are redefined to provide an opportunity to give recognition, direction, and feedback to an employee regarding his work on special projects (for example, Lean Six Sigma projects). This type of feedback promotes both extrinsic and intrinsic motivation. It provides extrinsic motivation in the giving of valuable feedback on special projects. It stimulates intrinsic motivation through the joy of a special project well done.

All the training steps in the *Training (Vocational Skills)* section of Figure 2.1 are redefined to identify each employee's needs for training through the empowerment process, that is, each employee receives the training required to turn the SDSA and PDSA cycles, or to use the DMAIC or DMADV models for process improvement. This is a source for extrinsic motivation, and definitely a major source for stimulating intrinsic motivation. It is fundamental to effective Lean Six Sigma management.

The *forecast employment requirements* step of the *Human Resources Planning* section, the *locate qualified candidates* step of the *Recruitment* section, the *select hire* step of the *Selection* section, and the *fired* and *layoff* steps of the *Terminations* section of Figure 2.1 are redefined to provide an equitable, objective, defensible system that satisfies the requirement of the 1964 Civil Rights Act and the Equal Opportunity Commission guidelines of 1966 and 1970. This is accomplished by committing to the values and spirit inscribed in the law, not just by conforming to the law. Terminations are extremely powerful extrinsic motivators to the individual threatened with termination. However, it can also be a major source of collateral damage to other employees doing a good job, but who now become fearful of losing their jobs. That is, this application of an extrinsic motivator can actually crush intrinsic motivation in the individuals surrounding the employee being terminated.

The *resolve personal problems* and *improve employee performance* steps of the *Employee Relations* section of Figure 2.1 are redefined to provide a channel for communication that otherwise would probably not occur. This can be accomplished by all employees in an organization by asking and answering the following questions:

- With whom is it important to maintain communication?
- For what purpose should I maintain communication?
- With what frequency should I maintain communication?
- In what kind of setting, format, or agenda, should I maintain communication?

Answers to the above questions should promote the flow of information and knowledge into channels of communication between people in organizations. These types of communications can provide powerful extrinsic and intrinsic motivation to employees.

2.2.4 Conclusion

It is important to realize that all the above processes form an interdependent system of processes. It does not make sense to adopt a new process for providing employees with a basis for salary and bonuses and not provide a process for identifying needs for training, education, and skill or career development. To do so may create a monster worse than the existing system of performance appraisal. For example, guaranteeing salary based on seniority without any process to improve the employee or organizational processes (PDSA cycle or DMAIC model) could be a formula for disaster.

Chapter 3

Working Conditions

3.1 Introduction

Have you ever said to yourself: "Don't look at the clock, just wait 15 more minutes before you look at the clock; it will be closer to lunch time. Yech! I looked at the clock. It's only 10:20. I'm so bored! I hate this job." In other words, when you think about going to work, do you think about being bored, frustrated, bullied by your supervisor, and just depressed? If the answer to any of the above questions is yes, and the pain of work is really bad, then there is some potentially good news. You may be able to change your situation at work. This chapter describes work in a Lean Six Sigma organization. It may help you decide if you want to support your organization's Lean Six Sigma process.

This chapter addresses several common problematic working conditions and their solutions in a Lean Six Sigma organization; they include: (1) poor training; (2) slogans, exhortations, and targets that demand higher levels of productivity; (3) work standards (quotas and piecework) on the factory floor; (4) fear; (5) barriers that rob the hourly worker of his or her right to pride of workmanship; and (6) lack of education and self-improvement efforts; see Deming (1986 and 1994) and Gitlow, Oppenheim, Oppenheim, and Levine (2004).

3.2 Poor Training

Employees are an organization's most important asset; they make the use of capital efficient and effective. Organizations must make long-term commitments to employees that include the opportunity to take joy in their work. This requires training in job skills.

Effective training changes the skill distribution for a job skill, as shown in Figure 3.1. Figure 3.1 shows the job skills distribution shifting from the fat curve on the left to the skinny curve on the right because of effective job skills training. Management must understand the capability of the current training process (including the current distribution of job skills) to improve the future distribution of job skills. Data, not guesswork or opinion, should be used to guide the training plans for employees.

Figure 3.2 shows a worker's daily production for 100 days before and after training. And Figure 3.3 shows dot-plots for the before and after training daily production data presented in Figure 3.2. Each dot represents one day's output. As you can see, the training program was extremely effective in shifting the distribution of the employee's output. As Figure 3.3 reveals, training increased the average output from approximately 19 per day to approximately 45 per day, and reduced day-to-day variation.

Training is a part of everyone's job and should include formal class work, experiential work, and instructional materials. Training courseware must take into consideration how the trainee learns and the speed at which the trainee learns. People

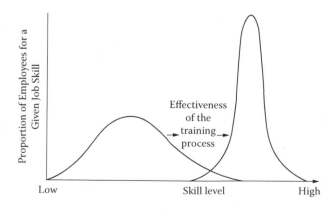

Figure 3.1   Distribution of job skills.

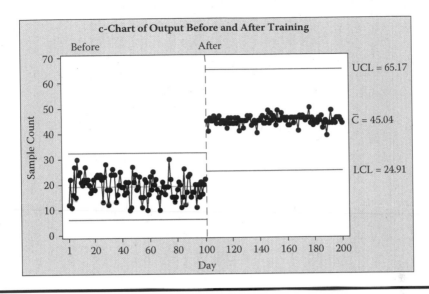

Figure 3.2   Daily production output for a worker before and after training.

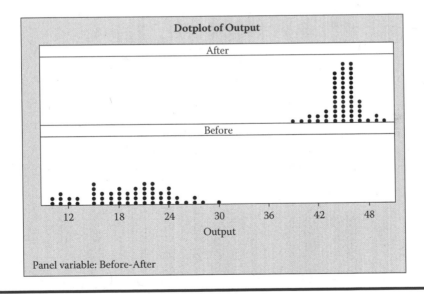

Figure 3.3   Current (before) and improved (after) skill distributions.

learn in several ways, some by doing, watching, listening, reading, or writing, to name a few.

Training should utilize statistical methods that indicate when an employee reaches a state of statistical control; that is, only common causes of variation are present in the key indicator(s) used to measure the employee's output; see the "After" section of the c-chart in Figure 3.2. If an employee is not in statistical control with respect to a job skill, then more training of the type the trainee is receiving will be beneficial. However, if an employee is in a state of statistical control with respect to a job characteristic, then more training of that type will not be beneficial; the employee has learned all that is possible from the training program.

You can support your organization's Lean Six Sigma efforts by willingly, and with good spirit, participating in Lean Six Sigma activities. As your skill distribution moves to the right as in Figure 3.1, you will experience less problems at work and feel more joy in work.

3.3 Slogans, Exhortations, and Targets That Demand Higher Levels of Productivity

Slogans, exhortations, and targets do not help to form a plan or method for the improvement or innovation of a process, product, or service. They do not operationally define process metrics in need of improvement or innovation. Slogans, exhortations, and targets are meaningless without methods to achieve them.

In general, targets are set arbitrarily by someone for someone else. If a target does not provide a method to achieve it, it is a meaningless plea. Examples of slogans, exhortations, and targets that do not help anyone do a better job include the following:

- ■ Do It Right The First Time.
- ■ Safety Is Job Number 1.
- ■ Zero Defects.
- ■ Just Say No.

These kinds of targets do not represent action items for employees; rather, they show management's wishes for a desired result. How, for example, can an employee "do it right the first time" without a method? People's motivation can be destroyed by slogans.

Slogans, exhortations, and targets shift responsibility for improvement and innovation of the system from management to the worker. The worker is powerless to make improvements to the system. This causes resentment, mistrust, and other negative emotions.

3.4 Work Standards (Quotas and Piecework) on the Factory Floor

Work standards and *piecework* are names given to a practice that can have devastating effects on quality and productivity.

A work standard is a specified level of performance determined by someone other than the worker who is actually performing the task. The effects of work standards are, in general, negative. They do not provide a road map for improvement, and they prohibit good supervision and training. In a system of work standards, workers are blamed for problems beyond their control. In some cases, work standards actually encourage workers to produce defectives to meet a production quota. This robs workers of their pride and denies them the opportunity to produce high-quality goods, and thus, to contribute to the stability of their employment.

A consultant was working in a factory that produced corrugated board boxes for packaging wet vegetables/fruit and raw meat. The boxes need a waxed inner coat to prevent moisture from destroying the box. During a plant tour, the consultant and the plant manager observed a worker feeding flat sheets of corrugated board into the waxing machine. The worker was going at an extremely fast rate. The consultant was impressed until he noticed that most of the boxes were not waxed properly, that is, they had dull spots — areas without shiny wax. The consultant asked the plant manager about the situation, and the plant manager shrugged his shoulders and said, "It's beyond my control." The consultant was surprised because the plant manager is ultimately responsible for the quality of the product. So the consultant asked him, "What do you mean, it's beyond your control? You're the plant manager." The plant manager said, "The employee is in the union, and the union contract states that he gets paid on a piecework rate. He can produce a much higher volume, and make more money, if he feeds in the corrugated sheets improperly, than if he feeds them in properly." The consultant said, "You mean that the worker is rewarded for producing defective product because the piecework clause in the union contract speaks only to quantity and not to quality?" The plant manager responded, "Yep!" And so it frequently goes with piecework.

Work standards are negotiated values that have no relationship to the capability of a process. When work standards are set too high or too low, there are additional devastating effects. Setting work standards too high increases pressure on workers and results in the production of more defectives. Worker morale and motivation decrease because the system encourages the production of defectives. Setting work standards too low also has negative effects. Workers who have met their quota spend the end of the day doing nothing; their morale is also destroyed.

Work standards are frequently used for budgeting, planning, and scheduling, and provide management with invalid information on which to base decisions. Planning, budgeting, and scheduling would improve greatly if they were based on the actual computed average for a stable process (a process with only common causes of variation).

3.5 Fear

There are two kinds of negative reactive behaviors: (1) fear and (2) anxiety. Fear is a reaction to a situation in which the person experiencing the fear can identify its source. Anxiety is a reaction to a situation in which the person experiencing the anxiety cannot identify its source. One can remove the source of fear because it is known. One cannot remove the source of anxiety because it is not known.

Fear has a profound impact on those working in an organization and, consequently, on the functioning of the organization. On an individual level, fear can cause physical and physiological disorders such as a rise in blood pressure or an increase in heart rate. Behavioral changes, emotional problems, and physical ailments often result from fear and stress generated in work situations, as do drug and alcohol abuse, absenteeism, and burnout. These maladies impact heavily on any organization. An employee subjected to a climate dominated by fear experiences poor morale, poor productivity, stifling of creativity, reluctance to take risks, and reduced motivation. The economic loss to an organization from fear is immeasurable, but huge.

A data-driven management system will not work in a fear-filled environment. This is because people in the system will view data as a vehicle for policing and judging, rather than a method that provides opportunities for improvement. Frequently, worker bees will manipulate data so they do not get into trouble with their supervisors. An example is a production worker who has exceeded his quota this month and hides the extra production so he can save it for the next period, just in case.

Fear emanates from the lack of job security, possibility of physical harm, ignorance of company goals, shortcomings in hiring and training, poor supervision, lack of operational definitions, failure to meet quotas, blame for the problems of the system (fear of being below average and being punished), and faulty inspection procedures, to name a few causes. Management is responsible for changing the organization to eliminate the causes of fear.

3.6 Barriers That Rob the Hourly Worker of His Right to Pride of Workmanship

Lean Six Sigma management promotes the idea that people are born with the right to find joy in their work. Unfortunately, very few people are able to feel joy in their work because of poor management. Management must remove the barriers that prevent employees from finding joy in their work.

In the current system of management, there are many barriers to joy in work. Some of these barriers are:

1. Employees not understanding their company's mission and manager's expectations
2. Employees being forced to act as automatons that are not allowed to think or use their skills
3. Employees being blamed for problems of the system
4. Employees having to work with hastily designed products and inadequately tested prototypes
5. Employees receiving inadequate supervision and training
6. Employees having to use faulty equipment, materials, and methods
7. Employees being rewarded and punished solely on results

Organizations will reap tremendous benefits when management removes barriers to joy in work.

3.7 Lack of Education and Self-Improvement Efforts

Education and self-improvement are important vehicles for the continuous improvement of employees, both professionally and personally. Executives are obligated to educate and improve themselves *and* their people to optimize the organization.

The purpose of training is to improve one's job skills, while the purpose of education is to improve one's mind, body, and spirit. Organizational policy frequently provides resources to train employees, but not to educate them. For example, a maintenance worker who is sent to a seminar to improve his knowledge about maintenance methods is receiving training. The same worker who is being sent to a seminar on basketball strategy is receiving education. Organizations frequently pay for the former, but not the latter. Dr. Deming once overheard two managers talking about how training seminars are great but that it would be crazy to send workers to educational seminars. One manager said to the other that Deming would have them pay for workers to get basketball lessons. Deming's comment was, "Teach them teamwork." And there you have it, you never know what the unintended benefits of education will be to the development of a worker's job-related skills.

Chapter 4

Behavior and Relationships

4.1 Types of Individual Behavior

It is critical to your professional development that you learn (see Tucker-Ladd, 2005), if you do not already know, appropriate interpersonal behavioral skills. These skills help you handle difficult situations by exercising deliberate control over the outcome of the situation. Professional inter-personal behavior involves recognizing your own weaknesses and working to overcome them, not by changing other people or the environment, but by primarily changing your own behaviors, feelings, skills, and thoughts.

There are several kinds of behavior, including assertive, passive, and aggressive. Assertive people stand up for their rights without violating the rights of others. They tactfully, justly, and effectively express needs and wants, and opinions and feelings. Passive people are weak, compliant, and self-sacrificing. Aggressive people are self-centered, inconsiderate, hostile, and arrogantly demanding of others.

Frequently, passive people want to be nice and not create trouble; consequently, they suffer in silence and get frustrated at their lot in life. If a passive person permits an aggressive person to take advantage of him- or herself, the passive person is not only cheating him- or herself, but is also enabling dysfunctional behavior in the aggressive person.

4.1.1 Purpose of Assertive Behavior

Assertive behavior is frequently helpful in coping with fear, shyness, passivity, and even anger. Consequently, it is appropriate for a broad spectrum of situations. Assertive behavior involves:

- Stating what is on your mind, asking for things, requesting favors, and generally insisting that your rights be respected as a significant, equal human being
- Stating negative feelings such as complaints, resentment, disagreement, and refusing requests from other people
- Demonstrating positive feelings such as joy or attraction, and giving compliments
- Asking why and questioning authority or tradition, not to rebel, but to assume responsibility for asserting your share of control of the situation
- Starting, participating in, changing, and stopping conversations
- Resolving irritations before you get angry and feel aggressive

4.1.2 Steps toward Assertive Behavior

Assertive behavior can be developed and practiced using the four-step method discussed below. Remember that assertive behavior requires practice.

4.1.2.1 Step 1

The first step toward assertive behavior involves identifying situations in which you exhibit passive or aggressive behavior. Recognize that you have the right to change from being a passive or aggressive person to being an assertive person. Please answer the following questions:

Do you have difficulty saying "no?"	(Yes/No)
Do you see yourself as unassertive?	(Yes/No)
Are you depressed?	(Yes/No)
Do you have many physical ailments?	(Yes/No)
Do you frequently complain about work?	(Yes/No)

If you answered "yes" to one or more of the above questions, then you may have difficulty being an assertive person.

Table 4.1   Part of Marsha's Diary of Unassertive Behavior for Two Weeks

Episode No.	Date	Description of Unassertive Episode
1	1/15/05	Cannot say no
2	1/15/05	Let my son get away with murder
3	1/15/05	Can't say no
4	1/15/05	Can't say no
5	1/15/05	Can't say no
6	1/15/05	Can't ask for simple directions
7	1/15/05	Can't say no
8	1/15/05	Can't say no
…		…
124	1/28/05	Can't say no
125	1/28/05	Let my son get away with murder
126	1/28/05	Can't say no

You will continue to be an unassertive person until you decide to change your behavior. A common aid for identifying the situations in which you are unassertive (intimidated, compliant, passive), or situations in which others are aggressive (demanding, whiny, bitchy), is to keep an "unassertiveness diary." You can use a control chart (c-chart) to determine if the number of unassertive episodes you experience per week is a stable and predictable, although possible unacceptable, system of behavior. If it is, then you can use a Pareto diagram to identify the most frequent type of unassertive episode.

For example, Marsha keeps a daily diary of her unassertive behavior for a two-week period; see Table 4.1. Table 4.2 shows the number of unassertive episodes per day taken from Table 4.1 before a change to Marsha's behavioral response to unassertive episodes. Figure 4.1 is a control chart of the number of unassertive episodes per day for the period from January 15 through 28, 2005. It shows that the number of unassertive episodes per day is a stable and predictable process with an average of nine episodes per day, an upper control limit (UCL) of 18 episodes per day, and a lower control limit (LCL) of zero (0) unassertive episodes per day. Figure 4.2 is a Pareto diagram with type of unassertive episode on the *x*-axis and frequency on the *y*-axis. The Pareto diagram highlights "can't say no" as the most frequent type of unassertive behavior.

Marsha decides to use an "I" message (discussed later in this chapter) to improve her ability to appropriately "say no." Figure 4.3 is a control chart showing

Table 4.2   Daily Count of Number of Unassertive Episodes

Date	No. of Unassertive Episodes
1/15/2005	11
1/16/2005	9
1/17/2005	9
1/18/2005	8
1/19/2005	7
1/20/2005	9
1/21/2005	9
1/22/2005	11
1/23/2005	7
1/24/2005	13
1/25/2005	9
1/26/2005	6
1/27/2005	7
1/28/2005	11
Total	126

the effectiveness of Marsha's use of the "I" message in the two-week period from January 29 to February 11, 2005. The "I" message seems to be an effective method for reducing the incidences of unassertive episodes in Marsha's life. "Can't say no" has shifted to a minor second-place problem.

An analysis of the January 29 through February 11 "unassertive episode" data shows the largest bar to be, "Let my son get away with murder"; see Figure 4.4. Marsha may have to develop a special "I" message for her son.

Remember that there are situations in which a sudden change from passive to assertive behavior may be problematic. For example, your boss might be upset and fire you, your spouse might be confused and want a separation or divorce, or your best friend might get upset and start to cry. For the above extreme situations, try to develop a plan for a slow and gradual change in your behavior. In any event, you should talk to your family, friends, and associates about your decision to become an assertive person. Surprisingly, the people around you may be supportive of your efforts.

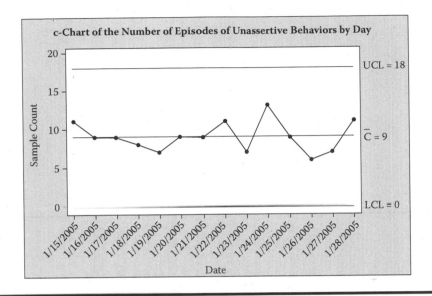

Figure 4.1   Marsha's c-chart of unassertive behavior per day.

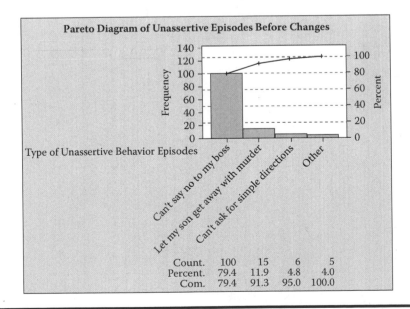

Figure 4.2   Marsha's Pareto diagram of unassertive behavior.

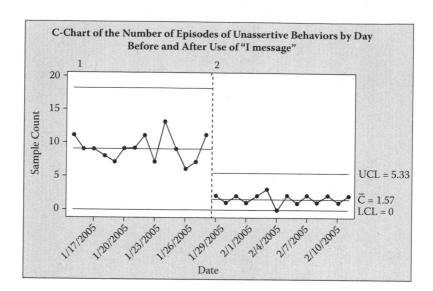

Figure 4.3   Marsha's before and after c-chart.

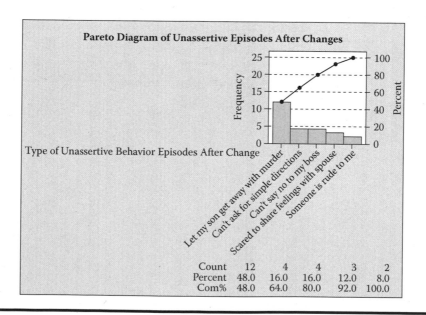

Figure 4.4   Marsha's after Pareto diagram.

4.1.2.2 Step 2

The second step toward assertive behavior involves preparing a response to a category of unassertive episodes from a Pareto diagram; see Figures 4.2 and 4.4. An "I" message is one type of assertive response to an unassertive episode. It is used to help people accept responsibility for their feelings. A useful rule is that "if you are confronted with an unassertive or aggressive episode, use an I-message."

An "I" message has four parts: (1) it states "I," "me," or "my"; (2) it expresses a feeling; (3) it may describe the other person's behavior that is related to your feelings; and (4) it may indicate what you would like to see changed. A typical format for an "I" message is: "I *(you)* feel *(your emotional state)* when *(the condition(s) that creates your emotional state)*. Would you please *(the desired condition)*?" For example, "I get frustrated when you arrive late for our weekly meetings because it makes me feel that you do not respect the value of my time. Please be on time from now on. Thanks."

You must do five things to effectively communicate your feelings about an unassertive or aggressive episode using an "I" message; they are:

1. Recognize the unassertive or aggressive episode.
2. Interpret the situation (what is going on?).
3. Understand your feelings about the episode.
4. Make an "I" message about the episode.
5. Deliver the "I" message to its recipient.

You may decide to hide, reject, deny, or transform into physical symptoms your feelings about the unassertive or aggressive episode. Or, you may decide to blame another person for a particular unassertive or aggressive episode and demand that he or she change his or her behavior. On the other hand, if you do not like how you feel with respect to an unassertive or aggressive episode, you can attempt to change your feelings.

If you are unaware of your feelings concerning an unassertive or aggressive episode or are not able to express your feelings, then you are likely to use a "you" statement. Table 4.3 shows some examples of "you" statements and "I" statements.

Many "you" statements are used to control, intimidate, or put down another person. They are not statements made by assertive people; they are messages sent by manipulative people.

If you use "we," "it," or "they" messages to depersonalize your comment or vaguely conceal your feelings, you are avoiding personal responsibility for a situation. For example, you are not taking personal responsibility for your feelings if you use "we" to create the impression that other people share your view of a situation, when in fact no one has authorized you to speak for them. Table 4.4 provides examples of "we" and "I" messages.

Table 4.3 Examples of "You" and "I" Statements

"You" Statements	*"I" Statements*
Blaming: "You make me so frustrated."	"I feel frustrated when you ...."
Judging or labeling: "You are an idiot."	"I feel foolish when you criticize me in public."
Accusing: "You hate me!"	"I feel neglected when you speak to me in that tone of voice."
Ordering: "You shut up!"	"I feel annoyed when you call me names and make fun of me."
Questioning: "Why did you do that?"	"I feel bad when you do that."
Arguing: "You don't know what you are talking about."	"I feel convinced it is this way."
Sarcasm: "Of course, you are an expert!"	"I would like you a lot more if you were a bit more humble."
Approving: "You're an expert."	"I am impressed with your knowledge."
Disapproval: "You are a rotten person."	"I feel crushed when you seem only interested in spending my money."
Threatening: "You better ...."	"I'd like it if you'd ...."
Moralizing: "You should ...."	"I think it would be fair for you to ...."
Treating: "You need to rest and ...."	"I'd like to be helpful to you."
Supporting: "It will get better."	"I'm sorry you feel ...."
Analyzing: "You can't stand to leave your mother!"	"I'm disappointed that you are so reluctant to leave ...."

The previous example shows that your personal opinions can sound like facts if you use "am" or "is" — for example, "You are ...," or "It is ...". Additionally, "am" or "is" messages imply the whole person is a certain way, forever. For example: "You are a moron" says that the person has no intelligence at all. This is an over-generalization. It would be better to say, "I resent it when you make plans without asking me what I want to do."

4.1.2.3 Step 3

The third step toward assertive behavior involves practicing *giving assertive responses to your most common types of unassertive or aggressive episodes.*

Table 4.4   Examples of "We" and "I" Statements

"We," "It," "They" Statements	"I" Statements
"The team doesn't think ...."	"I don't think the team believes ...."
"The team is attempting to help you with your problem."	"I want to help you with your problem, but I'm having a hard time understanding the problem."
"This restaurant is depressing me."	"I am depressed."
"This movie is a waste of my time."	"I feel I am wasting my time."

Workshop: Select a problem situation in which you are repetitively passive or aggressive. Write out an "I" message for responding to the situation. For example, "I feel frustrated because you have shown up late to two of our last three meetings. Please show up on time for our meetings in the future. Thank you."

Practice your "I" messages with a friend using role play for your most common unassertive or aggressive episodes. You will quickly find out that regardless of how calm and tactful you are, your new assertive behavior will sometimes be viewed as an attack on the other person involved. You should prepare yourself for possible strong reactions to your assertive behavior; for example, the other person involved might:

- Get angry at you
- Say nasty things to you
- Counterattack and criticize you
- Seek revenge against you
- Become sick or cry to evoke your feelings of guilt
- Suddenly become passive with you

If you choose to practice "I" messages with a friend, ask them to act out the more likely reactions. Frequently, explaining your behavior to the other person involved and being firm about your new assertive behavior will handle the situation.

You may find yourself falling into old passive or aggressive behaviors when you are criticized for your assertive behavior; for example, you might:

- Be sarcastic
- Procrastinate
- Get mad
- Be slow to get work done
- Be late for appointments
- Get quiet

- Be whiny
- Criticize back
- Do anything that drives him or her up a wall ("Oh, I didn't know that was bothering you.")

Try not to behave in an "I count, you don't count" position because that is aggressive behavior. Also, try not to behave in a "You count, I don't count" position because that is passive behavior. Attempt to behave in a "We both count equally" position. A "We both count equally" position includes the following elements:

- Listen carefully, and ask for clarification, until you understand the other person's views. Focus your comments on his or her main point(s), and ask, "What is it that bothers you about …?"
- If the criticism is valid, acknowledge the criticism. You can give honest explanations ("I was stuck in traffic," if it is valid) but do not make excuses ("I was stuck in traffic," if it is not valid).

If part of the criticism is true, acknowledge that part of the criticism. For example, "You could be right about *that part* of what you said," or "I understand how you feel about *that part* of what you said." These last two comments are avoiding the basic unassertive or aggressive episode.

Some people will not accept your saying "no" as an answer; that is, they refuse to acknowledge your reasonable assertive behavior. Sometimes you have to repeat a message many times to increase the likelihood that the other person involved in the unassertive episode will hear it. Sometimes you can use *the "broken record" technique to* be *heard by the other person*. For example, you calmly and firmly repeat a concise statement multiple times until the other person understands your message; for example:

- "I want you to arrive at the meeting at 1:00 p.m."
- "I am not happy with my new sport jacket; I want to return it for a complete refund."
- "I don't want to go out tonight; I want to stay home."

Repeat the same statement until the other person involved in the unassertive or aggressive episode leaves you alone, regardless of the excuses, diversions, or arguments.

There are two additional techniques that are useful when confronting difficult situations and people. You use these techniques when the communication is breaking down; for example:

- The topic has shifted to something other than resolving the unassertive or aggressive episode.

- Both participants in the unassertive or aggressive episode are losing control of their emotions.
- Both participants in the unassertive or aggressive episode cannot resolve the episode.

Two techniques for dealing with these situations are described below:

> *Technique 1.* Shift the focus from the unassertive or aggressive episode at hand to what is currently happening between you and the other person; for example:
>   - "We are both getting upset; let's try to stay reasonable."
>   - "We have drifted off the subject; can we go back to _____?"
> *Technique 2.* Delay the time for dealing with the unassertive or aggressive episode at hand by taking a break:
>   - "That's an important point; give me a chance to mull it over. Can we take an hour break?"
>   - "I need to sleep on that; can we talk tomorrow at lunch?"

4.1.2.4 Step 4

The fourth step toward assertive behavior involves *using assertive behavior in actual unassertive or aggressive episodes.* Begin using assertive behavior in the situations you have practiced with your role-playing friend. As you become more confident, you can attempt to deal with more stressful situations. Modify your assertive behavior as appropriate. You might consider keeping a diary of your unassertive or aggressive episodes and analyze it with a control chart and Pareto diagram.

Note that personal belief systems are frequently major contributors to unassertive behavior. Some examples of values and beliefs that can be dysfunctional include never be selfish, never make mistakes, never be emotional, never second-guess people, never interrupt people, never complain, and never brag. These values and beliefs can contribute to being a passive person. No personal belief system is rational in all situations; for example, sometimes you can put your needs above the needs of others, occasionally you can make mistakes, sometimes you can be emotional, if appropriate you can state your feelings, if needed you can ask for help, and sometimes you can say "no."

If after using the above four-step method, the person you are interacting with is still negative about your developing assertive behavior, then you may want to reevaluate your relationship. This can be very scary.

4.1.3 *Personal Discipline*

Why can some people accomplish so much and stay focused on a task, while others are battered by daily events and get little accomplished; see TribuneIndia.com (1999). Those battered souls have a long laundry list of distractions and excuses for their poor performance, including crises, miscommunications, stress, pressure, management style, poor training, lack of supervision, short deadlines, and inadequate resources, to name a few.

Why do we accept these distractions and excuses as inevitable? Why do we choose to suffer on a daily basis? Why do we not have the insight and energy to realize that we have options? Why do we think that changing our lives for the better will exact an enormous and painful price? Why do we choose to do nothing and remain in pain? Why do we not realize that personal discipline can make an enormous difference in how we react to the circumstances that define our lives?

One possible answer to the last question is that five common myths keep us down and prevent us from transforming into all we can be. The myths are:

1. People who are successful are just lucky.
2. People cannot change the way they think and interact with the world.
3. People who exhibit personal discipline are not free to pursue their dreams and desires.
4. People cannot affect their future.
5. People who exhibit personal discipline are perfectionists.

The above myths are impediments to making our lives better. Learning how to eliminate these impediments is the focus of this section.

4.1.3.1 Debunking Myth 1

People with personal discipline are organized and focused on achieving their goals. They do not flip-flop from one thing to another and thereby lose focus on their primary mission. People with personal discipline can say "no" to attractive distracters, wasters of their time, and unnecessary interruptions that would pull them off their focused path. They understand their available options and which options will best move them toward their goals. This is how people with personal discipline accomplish so much.

4.1.3.2 Debunking Myth 2

People with personal discipline can change the way they think by studying the literature and opinions of experts that are relevant to their lives. They do not have to follow the pack. Importantly, their personal esteem is based on their internal psychological make-up (internal focus), not on how they are perceived by the people (external focus) and circumstances that make up their world.

4.1.3.3 Debunking Myth 3

People with personal discipline have the time to pursue their goals because they are focused on their goals, they are not easily distracted, and they know how to prioritize their time. They are free to pursue their dreams and desires because they can focus and plan.

4.1.3.4 Debunking Myth 4

People with personal discipline can affect their future by being proactive — not reactive. They do not have to wait for "a white knight" to save them, or a miracle to happen. Winning the lottery is not the only path to salvation. Personal discipline is the path to positively affecting one's future. It requires knowledge, guts, determination, and focus.

4.1.3.5 Debunking Myth 5

People with personal discipline do not demand perfection, but constantly try to improve their situation. They have the energy and focus to constantly keep on improving.

You can develop your personal discipline using appropriate tools and methods. These tools and methods are discussed below. There are different tools and methods for improving personal discipline, depending on whether you want to impact it before, during, or after a breach in personal discipline.

The methods used to impact a breach in personal discipline *before it occurs* are discussed below. Keep a diary of the situations leading up to the breach in personal discipline, identify the precursors of the breach, and then change or avoid the precursors of the breach to maintain personal discipline. Break the situations leading up to the breach as early as possible.

- Study the literature (use Internet search engines and go to the library) or talk to experts about acceptable alternatives to the breach in personal discipline; for example, exercise instead of eating lunch. Practice the alternative behaviors.
- Control your environment by eliminating temptations that provoke the breach in personal discipline; for example, buy fruits for dessert, not sweets.
- Practice "prevention behaviors" and "resistance behaviors"; for example, take five deep breaths before responding to a potential problematic situation.
- Focus on positive and negative long-range consequences of the breach; for example, imagining how you will feel the next day if you take a particular action.

The method used to impact a breach in personal discipline *while it is occurring* is described below:

- Observe and record the frequency and intensity of your breach behavior using a diary. Set SMART goals for eliminating your breach behavior. SMART is an acronym for Specific, Measurable, Achievable, Reasonable, and Time Bound. Evaluate your progress toward your SMART goals.

- Recall and record data before the breach, as well as observe and record data after the breach.
- Analyze the before and after data to understand how you respond (after data) to different stimuli (before data). Use this information to develop a method for effectively changing your reactions to the before data; that is, redefine your responses to a breach behavior as a "before the behavior occurs" scenario. Recall how Ralph used a control chart and a Pareto diagram to record, analyze, and improve his "relationship with women" process.

The methods used to impact a breach in personal discipline *after it has occurred* are shown below:

- Write a contract that includes self-rewarding for the desired behavior. Initially, use immediate and continuous reinforcement for the desired behavior, then reduce the reward to intermittent rewards, and then finally, eliminate the reinforcement.
- Provide yourself with something unpleasant, or remove something pleasant, to make up for breaking the rules in your personal improvement plan.

4.2 Selected Types of Relationships

There are two types of relationships at work that are discussed in this section. Both types can make you happy or miserable; they are (1) boss–subordinate relationships (for example, mentoring boss, visionary boss *versus* difficult boss, harassing boss, incompetent boss, unconcerned boss, micro-managing boss) and (2) co-worker relationships (for example, team player co-worker, watching-your-back co-worker *versus* bullying co-worker, inept co-worker).

4.2.1 Boss–Subordinate Relationships

There are two fundamental supervision styles: (1) the "hands-off" style and (2) the "hands-on" style, also called micro-managing (see Mayo Clinic). The hands-off style gives you space to decide how best to accomplish your work; that is, it provides minimal supervision. If you can work with minimal supervision, this style is great; but many people require more supervision to exhibit effective performance on the job. If there is a mismatch between your boss's style of supervision and your desired style of supervision, it will create stress in your work. You can try speaking with your boss about the amount of supervision she gives you. This may decrease your stress at work. If this conversation works for you, then your problem is solved. If not, then you will have to try another tactic. One tactic may be to learn the assertive behavior techniques that were discussed previously in this book.

If you work for a micro-manager (the constant "hands-on" style of supervision), you will likely experience a supervisor who always looks over your shoulder and demands that you work exactly to his or her specifications and time frame. One three-step tactic you can use to improve your relationship with a micro-managing boss is:

1. *Develop a Gantt chart for your next work assignment.* The next time your supervisor gives you an assignment, develop a work plan that includes the tasks to be done, who is responsible for each task, and a timeline for each task. This is called a "Gantt chart." It is used to construct a schedule for the project and list any milestones. It is a bar chart that plots tasks and sub-tasks against time. Once a list of tasks and sub-tasks has been created for a project, then responsibilities can be assigned for each task or sub-task. Next, beginning and finishing dates can be scheduled for each task and sub-task. Finally, any milestones relevant to a task or sub-task are placed on the Gantt chart. A generic Gantt chart is shown in Table 4.5.

2. *Use the Gantt chart to seek input from your boss on the progress of your assignment.* Get your boss's feedback on your Gantt chart at appropriate times, for example, when you are scheduled to complete a task or when you are running over on a task. Listen to your boss' concerns and act accordingly.

3. *Follow through on your Gantt chart.* "Gantt chart your work and work your Gantt chart." This is your new motto. You may be surprised how your micro-managing boss gets off your back due to his or her improved feedback on the status of your assignment. If your boss questions how you did one of your tasks, you can say, "We agreed on this task when we last reviewed the Gantt chart." If your boss is still micro-managing you, gently confront him or her using an "I" message.

Unfortunately, sometimes you cannot change your relationship with your boss, regardless of the reason. This is clearly an upsetting situation. You are driving your boss nuts and he is driving you nuts. This is a classic "lose-lose" situation. If you find yourself in such a "lose-lose" situation, focus on what is within your control; for example:

Table 4.5 Generic Gantt Chart

Tasks	Responsibility	J	F	M	A	M	J	J	A	S	O	N	D	J	F	M	A	M	J	Milestones
Task 1																				
Sub-task 1a	HG	■	■																	
Sub-task 1b	HG			■	■	■														
Task 2	QZ					■	■													
Task 3																				
Sub-task 3a	QZ								■	■	■	■	■							
Sub-task 3b	RM														■	■				
Sub-task 3c	RM																	■	■	
Task 4																				

Time Line (Month)

- Think about the positive aspects of your job. Is your job worth the aggravation; or in other words, "Is the juice worth the squeeze?"
- Keep a positive attitude toward your work; for example, be a team player and work your Gantt chart.
- Realize that work is only part of your life; that is, maintain perspective. This can be difficult but it may help you.

If none of the above suggestions work for you, then you should consider looking for a new job, or at least a new boss. Do *not* quit your current job until you have a definite new job offer.

4.2.2 Co-Worker Relationships

Co-workers can be extremely important stakeholders in your life, if you let them and yourself embrace the relationship; see Leebov (1990). These relationships range from extremely positive and supportive to extremely negative and destructive. There are several simple principles that you can employ to develop more positive relationships with your co-workers, including:

- *Realize that people are different.* Every person is a unique individual with his or her own view of life. We should respect other people's views of a situation in which we are also a stakeholder.
- *Be a positive thinker.* Try not to dwell on the glass being half-empty — practice seeing the glass as half-full.
- *Acknowledge your co-workers.* Realize that your co-workers are human beings with their own views of the world and their own sets of problems and pressures. Sometimes a kind word or a smile from you can make the difference between your co-worker having a terrible day, a bearable day, or even a good day. Remember that frequently, what goes around, comes around. Acknowledge the good work of your colleagues.
- *Be an active listener.* You will never understand the dynamics of your relationships with your co-workers if you do not listen to what they have to say to you. Listening is an extremely positive act.
- *Be a team player.* Help your co-workers when they are in a tight spot without being a martyr, do your job to the best of your ability, respect your co-worker's priorities and time constraints, admit mistakes and apologize, if appropriate, realize that you have a life outside of work, and understand that things will not ever be perfect.

4.3 Selected Techniques for Improving Relationships

Edward de Bono developed many creative techniques that may be helpful to team members when resolving issues concerning difficult team members, creating alternative avenues for studying a problem and developing options for solving a defined problem. Three of de Bono's creative techniques are reiterated and illustrated in a team setting: Other People's Views (OPV); Consequences & Sequel (C&S); and Alternatives, Possibilities, and Choices (APC); see de Bono (1993).

4.3.1 Other People's Views (OPV)

OPV is a technique that can be used to identify all the stakeholders of a relationship (including future generations) and to imagine their views on the relationship. It can be used to consider all sides of a relationship. Two questions that you can ask yourself (or another stakeholder) of a relationship are:

- Who is affected by this relationship?
- What are the viewpoints of those affected by this relationship?

These questions may help you get a better feel for the different views of the relationship you should consider when trying to improve it. For example, a team is experiencing disruptions caused by a difficult team member. So, the team leader asks, "What is the viewpoint of the difficult team member, OPV?" The team members recognized that the difficult team member's boss is putting tremendous pressure on her to meet a quarterly sales quota. Fear of the quota is causing the team member to be stressed and resentful of any activity that takes her away from generating new sales. The team members recognize and empathize with her problem and help her meet her goal by pointing out sales opportunities she had not thought of due to her stressed condition. She makes some sales and is appreciative of her team members. She begins to be a positive source of energy for the team.

4.3.2 Consequences & Sequel (C&S)

C&S is a technique that can be used to determine the consequences of a decision about a relationship for a given time period. Several questions that you can ask yourself (or another stakeholder) about a decision made in respect to a relationship are:

- Will the decision work out?
- What are the benefits of the decision?
- What are the risks of the decision?
- What is the worst outcome?
- What is the best outcome?
- What is the expected outcome?
- What are the costs of the decision?
- How likely is this outcome?

For example, team members have a budget of $150,000 to complete a Lean Six Sigma project with a projected savings of $5,000,000 per year. As they move through the project, they realize that they can meet their project objective; but if they obtain an additional $100,000, they can double the hard revenue benefits of the project beyond what is expected from the define phase. They want the additional funds but are fearful of asking for them. They wonder if they should just do what is expected and forget going for the potentially dangerous home run. The team used C&S to resolve its problem by asking: "What is the risk of asking for more resources?"

The answer: Team members decide that the worst possible outcome of asking for more resources is that they will all get fired, or at least never promoted. Having verbalized their worst fear among themselves, they all realize that they are being irrational, especially given that the additional resources will double the results of their project. Next, the team members decide that the best possible outcome is that the champion and process owner are thrilled at the opportunity to double the results of the project with the additional expense. Further, as a result of their project work, they all get a bonus and a promotion. Finally, team members realize that the most realistic outcome is much closer to the best possible outcome than the worst possible outcome. They decide to request the additional funds. The champion and process owner are delighted at the prospect of the additional results. Problem solved!

4.3.3 Alternatives, Possibilities, and Choices (APC)

APC is a technique that can be used to expand the alternatives, possibilities, and choices concerning a decision to be made about a relationship. Questions that you can ask yourself (or another stakeholder) about a decision to be made in respect to a relationship are:

- What are alternative ways of looking at this relationship (APC)?
- What are alternative actions for making a decision about the relationship?
- What are alternative solutions for each decision about the relationship?
- What are alternative explanations for this relationship problem?

For example, the members of a Lean Six Sigma project team have identified the percentage of abandoned calls by month for the Accounts Receivable department as critical to customer quality characteristics (CTQ). They know that the relevant process is the phone answering process, but they are experiencing great difficulty thinking of alternative designs for this process that would reduce the percentage of abandoned calls by month. They have studied data on the process to no avail, and the same is the case for benchmarking other Accounts Receivable departments. Their frustration led them to a list of 70 possible generic ideas for improving a process; see Gitlow, Oppenheim, Oppenheim, and Levine (2004). Team members found that one of the 70 items was "shift demand." This seemed like a potentially valuable *alternative* change concept. The team members know from studying demand patterns that most of the abandoned calls occur between 10:00 a.m. and 2:00 p.m., Monday through Friday. The team members thought about how they could "shift demand" to a less busy time. The team leader asked two questions*:

- On average, how many times per year does a student telephone the Accounts Receivable office? Answer: About ten times per year.
- Do most students call ten times per year, or do most call zero times and a few call a hundred times per year? Answer: The latter.

Answer: At this point, the team members decided to install a system that required every clerk to enter the university student identification number into the computer. If a particular university student identification number showed more than nine calls in any given month, team members felt confident that they had identified a frequent caller. Consequently, they preemptively called the person at 8:00 a.m. to resolve any possible problems. Team members had shifted a sizeable portion of the calls away from busy times, and subsequently the "percentage of abandoned calls by month" dropped off dramatically. Problem is solved using an alternative concept!

---

* The author apologizes for not remembering the exact average and maximum number of calls per year per student. However, the point of the example is still valid.

4.4 Improving Team Behavior

It is critical to your professional development that you learn — if you do not already know — appropriate team behavior skills. A team is a small group of people with complementary skills who work for a common objective (mission) for which they hold themselves accountable; for example, people working on a Lean Six Sigma project team. It is critical that you learn how to work effectively and efficiently in a team setting; for example, knowing how to prevent getting stuck doing other team member's work, waiting for habitually late team members, or accepting disruptive behavior in team meetings.

No two people are exactly alike. People are different from each other in many ways. Some people are tall, others are short; some people are fat, others are skinny; some people respond well to authority, others act out; some people like math, others like language, and others like both; some learn quickly and others learn slowly; some learn by reading, while others learn by watching, and others by doing. A manager of people must understand the significance of these differences and use them when creating teams. Relevant individual differences are a necessary ingredient for a mature, fully functioning team because the team works under the assumption that the abilities of its members are complementary, not redundant. For example, it is desirable that a Lean Six Sigma project team have an expert in the theory and practice of the process under study, an expert in Lean Six Sigma theory and tools, an expert in the political and resource issues relevant to the process under study, an expert in information technology, an expert in finance, and an appropriate number of Lean Six Sigma savvy "process oriented" worker bees.

4.4.1 Stages of Team Behavior

The life of a team follows a prescribed cycle. The first stage in the life of a team is *forming*. Forming is the stage in which members get to know each other and seek to establish ground rules. This stage finishes with the awareness of being a group member. The second stage in the life of a team is *storming*. Storming is the stage in which members may have conflicting views of team goals, priorities, and how to move forward. Sometimes this manifests itself when team members resist direction from the group leader and show hostility. This stage finishes when conflicts are eliminated or resolved and members agree to an overall direction for the team facilitated by the team leader. The third stage of team development is *norming*. Norming is the stage in which team members begin to work together and develop interdependence for achieving the task and become more cohesive. This stage finishes when expectations are set regarding ways of doing things. The fourth stage in the life of a team is *performing*. Performing is the stage in which team members devote their energy to getting the job done and the team is functioning very well in accomplishing its agreed activities. The final stage in the life of a team is *adjourning*. Adjourning is the stage in which team members disband voluntarily or because the work is done. A well structured and facilitated team expends most of its time and energy in the performing stage.

4.4.2 Escalating "I" Messages for Improving Team Behavior

An escalating "I" message is a variant of a simple "I" message frequently used in a team format. If a simple "I" message fails to modify another person's or group's behavior, you can use an escalating "I" message. Team members use escalating "I" messages to deal with the following problematic team member behaviors:

- Slacker team member (shoddy work product, failure to provide timely work product)
- Dominating team member (e.g., does not stop talking, over-controlling personality)
- Argumentative team member
- Tardy team member
- Hostile team member
- Passive team member
- Inept team member (e.g., inability to perform needed work)
- Offensive team member (e.g., in terms of language, behavior, hygiene)

There are five steps of an escalating "I" message:

Step 1: Do nothing (non-intervention). Doing nothing is generally a bad way to proceed. It sets the stage for increasingly dysfunctional behavior on the part of the difficult team member.

Step 2: Off-line private conversation (minimal intervention). An off-line private conversation requires that the team leader be assertive, not passive-aggressive. An assertive team leader uses an "I" message to make a point. For example, "I am concerned about your tardiness to the team meetings because it makes me feel that you don't respect the value of my time. Please be on time from now on." A passive-aggressive team leader will let the problem go unresolved until it is so troublesome that it explodes in the team's face.

Step 3: Impersonal group time (low intervention). Impersonal group time utilizes a "we" message in a team meeting. A "we" message is just like an "I" message except that it comes from the entire team. For example, "We are concerned about your tardiness to our team meetings because it makes us feel that you don't respect the value of our time. Please be on time from now on."

Step 4: Off-line confrontation (medium intervention). An off-line confrontation by a team leader with a difficult team member reiterates the problem and solution, but it clearly states (politely with no sugar added to avoid confusion) the consequences of not conforming to the team's request. For example, "We are frustrated about your repeated tardiness to our team meetings because it makes us feel that you don't respect the value of our time. If you are not on time from now on, we will document your behavior in our team minutes for distribution to the champion and process owner."

Step 5: Expulsion from the group (high intervention). If at all possible, do not use this option! Expulsion from a group is a severe option and carries unknown consequences for the difficult employee and the team members. It is difficult to foresee how expelling a team member might play out years in the future.

Regardless of the stimulus from an individual or group, it is imperative that the team leader does not overreact (for example, hit the panic button) or under-react (for example, ignore the problem) to a problem. This requires an understanding of special and common causes of variation.

4.4.3 Conflict Resolution Skills for Improving Team Behavior

Conflict is part of the human condition. However, conflicts do not have to end with someone winning and someone losing. Assertive people can resolve conflicts with all participants still respecting each other. There are five conflict resolution styles:

1. *Avoiding or denying* a situation to stop conflict. This is a bad approach.
2. *Giving in* to stop conflict. This is another bad approach.
3. *Blaming* the other person to stop conflict. This is also a bad approach.
4. *Compromising* to stop conflict. This is a good approach if it creates a "no lose" solution at worst, or a "win–win" solution at best. However, it creates a "win-lose" or "lose-lose" solution if it is a bad approach.
5. *Integrating* all participants' differences and similarities to stop conflict. An integrative solution is built on the similarities of all participants. All participants are open and honest, not deceptive and manipulative. They build trust to develop a wise and workable solution. It is not easy, but this is a good approach.

There are many conflicts not subject to the fifth conflict state, for example, buying a used car. The salesperson wants a high price and you want a low price;

the two of you bargain, and then you may never see each other again. This kind of tough, unsympathetic, self-centered, often manipulative, deceptive, and hostile negotiating involves great skill. However, they are not the skills discussed in this book.

There are six steps for creating a solution to a conflict using the fifth conflict resolution style.

4.4.3.1 Step 1: View the Participants in the Conflict as Equals Trying to Solve a Problem to Their Mutual Advantage

"No-lose" or "win–win" conflict resolution strategies require that the participants enter the conflict as equals trying to identify a solution that both are happy with, or at least that neither is dissatisfied with. The participants should not think in terms of "win-lose" solutions. Conflict does not necessarily imply anger at each other. Conflict can provide an opportunity to strengthen a relationship and make all participants winners.

4.4.3.2 Step 2: Identify the Viewpoints of All Participants of the Conflict

The participants in a conflict should accept all the other participants' points of view as being valid. Each participant should enter the conflict with a respectful, open, and honest attitude. No one should campaign for his or her point of view, at the expense of another participant's point of view.

The participants in a conflict should collect information from each other to clarify the exact nature of the conflict. The "golden rule" of collecting data to find a positive solution to a conflict is: listen, listen, and listen. Do not begin by offering solutions; just listen and get all the facts. Do not assess blame. Be empathic and sympathetic. Be careful not to use offensive language. Describe the benefits and costs of a solution to the conflict to all participants. Consider past efforts to resolve the conflict. Consider the difference between what the other participants need (their "position") and what they really want (their "interest"). For example, suppose an employee asks for a pay raise (his or her "position") but the company cannot afford the pay raise. If you collected data and discovered that the employee likes his or her job, but his or her "interest" was to get transportation for her family, the company may be able to find a vehicle for the employee. Stating different demands or "positions" does not mean that your basic "interests" are irreconcilable.

Frequently, there are several *solutions* that will satisfy all the different interests of the participants of a conflict. Participants should avoid thinking in terms of only one solution. Also, participants should avoid feeling competitive. All of this takes time.

4.4.3.3 *Step 3: Develop Alternative Solutions for the Conflict That Result in "Win–Win" Situations, or at Least "No Lose" Situations*

All participants in the conflict should study the viewpoints and data concerning the conflict when creating "win–win" solutions, or at least "no lose" solutions.

4.4.3.3.1 Creating "Win–Win" Solutions to Conflicts

When creating "win–win" solutions to conflicts, people use their values and beliefs to define a conflict and develop a range of alternative solutions. Consider including the following values and beliefs into your decision-making process because they encourage "win–win" solutions:

- *Improve the process that makes results; do not just demand results.* Manage by improving processes to get results (process and results management); do not manage just to get results (results-only management). Process and results management promotes improvement and innovation of organizational processes. Highly capable processes facilitate prediction of the near future, and consequently a higher likelihood of achieving the desired results. Results-only management causes people to abuse processes to get their desired results, and ultimately things get worse. For example, do not just demand better grades from your child; rather, help your child figure out how to improve his or her studying process. As another example, do not just demand more productivity from your subordinate; rather, help your subordinate improve the process used to generate results using the PDSA cycle or the DMAIC model.
- *Balance intrinsic and extrinsic motivators; do not just use extrinsic motivators.* Manage to create a balance between intrinsic and extrinsic motivation for each individual; do not rely only on extrinsic motivation to stimulate people. Intrinsic motivation comes from the sheer joy of doing an act, for example, the joy from a job well done. It releases human energy that can be focused on the improvement and innovation of a process (job). Intrinsic motivation cannot be given to an individual. It comes entirely from within the person experiencing it. Extrinsic motivation comes from desire for reward or fear of punishment, for example, the feelings stimulated by receiving a bonus. It comes from someone else, not the individual experiencing it. Frequently, extrinsic motivation can restrict the release of energy from intrinsic motivation by judging and policing an individual.

  Managers can create a fertile environment for others to experience intrinsic motivation in two ways. First, managers can promote joy in work by empowering employees to improve the processes in which they work using the PDSA cycle or the DMAIC model. Second, managers can hire and assign people into job positions that suit their personality and abilities. People are more likely to experience intrinsic motivation if they are performing a job for which they are suited.

■ *Promote cooperation; do not compete if the aim of the system is not to win.* Manage to promote cooperation, not competition, if the aim of the system is not to win. If the aim of the system is to win, then competition makes sense. For example, when two professional baseball teams play each other, the aim is to win. However, if the aim of the system is not to win, then competition does not make sense. For example, if the aims of all the salespersons in an organization are to optimize revenues for the company, then competition does not make sense. Salespeople should cooperate by sharing selling tips and techniques, and not compete in events like sales contests because such contests stifle cooperation and the sharing of information. In a competitive environment, most people lose. The costs resulting from competition are unknown and unknowable, but they are huge.

■ *Optimize the whole system, not just your component of the system.* Manage to optimize the whole system, not just your component of the system. The whole system includes the interdependent system of stakeholders of an organization. Some stakeholders are investors, customers, employees, divisions, departments and areas within departments, suppliers, subcontractors, regulators, the community, and the environment. Intersystem competition causes individuals, subsystems, or stakeholders to optimize their own efforts at the expense of other stakeholders. This form of optimization seriously erodes overall system performance. For example, investors demanding a downsizing of employees in a year of record profit, or one department demanding resources that it knows could be better used in another department.

These values and beliefs are examined because they form the core assumptions of Lean Six Sigma management. They have been proven successful in many Lean Six Sigma endeavors.

The above four values and beliefs frequently provide a different lens for viewing many conflicts and create the opportunity to develop "win–win" solutions to such conflicts. However, if the above four values and beliefs do not generate one or more "win–win" solutions to a conflict, then the people involved must fall back to the development of "no lose" solutions to conflicts.

4.4.3.3.2 Creating "No Lose" Solutions to Conflict

A few good rules you can use to develop and select a "no lose" solution to a conflict episode include:

- Be open and willing to modify your solution(s).
- Be clear about the rationale behind your solution(s). Each participant in a conflict should describe the solution he or she wants. Each potential solution should be specific and not contain vague comments; for example, "I want clearer supervision." A more specific solution is: "I want to spend 30 minutes together at the start of every day so we can discuss my priorities for work."
- Consider the needs and wants of all participants in your solution(s). Do not insult or criticize the other participants; for example, do not say, "You are so uncommunicative." Do not push for solutions that are very difficult or impossible for the other participants in the conflict to live with, such as a change of feelings: "Accept my yelling at you in public."
- State your proposed solution(s) so that they are as pleasant as possible for the other participants to hear.
- Each participant presents his or her two best solutions and asks the other participants which solution they like best, or if they can improve upon one of the solutions. If another participant seems dissatisfied with one of your solutions, ask: "What would you do if you were me?"

4.4.3.4 Step 4: All Participants in the Conflict Review the "Win–Win" Solutions or Negotiate the Differences in Their Solutions to Create "No Lose" Solutions to the Conflict

"Win–win" solutions to a conflict do not require much discussion before they can be implemented due to their nature. However, "no lose" solutions to a conflict do require discussion of the different viewpoints present before they are implemented.

4.4.3.5 Step 5: Avoid the Common Pitfalls of "No Lose" Solutions

If a "win–win" solution is not possible, then the first common pitfall is to assume that there is one best "no lose" solution (usually yours) to the conflict. In most situations, a good "no lose" (compromise) solution benefits all participants in some way. The second common pitfall is not establishing a process for making decisions. If the participants in a conflict episode do not have a clear process for making decisions, then it is likely that they will resort to their old aggressive or passive behaviors. The third common pitfall is to misjudge the personality of one or more of the participants of the conflict episode. For example, you assume that you are dealing with a reasonable and dependable person who is willing to develop a "no lose" (compromise) solution, but discover too late that he or she is a manipulative shark. The fourth common pitfall is losing your patience with the process for developing a "no lose" solution.

4.4.3.6 Step 6: Try Out the "Win–Win" Solution or the Best "No Lose" Solution for a Limited Time Period

Participants in the conflict episode develop a plan for executing the solution. This means they identify: who does what, where, when, and how. Once the plan is developed, it can be put into action for a trial time period, and then it can be reevaluated as needed.

Chapter 5

Conclusion

Now that you have read this book, you may be asking, "What do I do now?" Well, the answer is best said in the punch line of an old joke. Here it goes...

A young man carrying a violin was lost in New York City. He stopped a taxi driver and asked, "Excuse me sir, but how do I get to Carnegie Hall?" The taxi driver looked at the young man, then at the violin, then at the young man. He said, "Practice, practice, practice!"

And so my reader, the answer to your question: "What do I do now?" has been answered — practice, practice, practice.

Thank you for reading this book. If you would like to know more about Lean Six Sigma management, see references by Gitlow, Levine, and Popovich (2006); Gitlow and Levine (2004); and Gitlow, Oppenheim, Oppenheim, and Levine (2004). Also visit HowardGitlow.com for free, detailed Lean Six Sigma case studies as well as other products and services.

Bibliography

de Bono, E. (1993), *Teach Your Child How to Think*, Penguin Group, New York.

Deming, W.E. (1994), *The New Economics for Industry, Government, Education, 2nd edition*, M.I.T. C.A.E.S., Boston, MA.

Deming, W.E. (1986), *Out of the Crisis*, M.I.T. C.A.E.S., Boston, MA.

Friedman, M. and Gitlow, H., A Lean Six Sigma Primer for CPAs, *The CPA Journal*, 72(11), 56–59, 2002.

Gitlow, H., Levine, D., and Popovich, E. (2006), *Design for Lean Six Sigma for Green Belts and Champions*, Financial Times/Prentice Hall, Saddle River, NJ.

Gitlow, H. and Levine, D. (2004), *Lean Six Sigma for Green Belts and Champions*, Financial Times/Prentice Hall, Saddle River, NJ.

Gitlow, H., Oppenheim, A., Oppenheim, R., and Levine, D. (2004), *Quality Management: Tools and Methods for Improvement*, Richard, D., Irwin Publishers, Ridgewood, IL.

Gitlow, H., Kellogg, S., and Kang, K. (1992–1993), "Process Tampering: An Analysis of On/Off Deadband Process Controlling," *Quality Engineering*, 5(2), 293–310.

Johnson, A., Widener, S., Gitlow, H., and, Popovich, E. (2006), Designing New Housing at the University of Miami: A "Lean Six Sigma" DMADV/DFSS Case Study, *Quality Engineering*, 18(3), 299–323.

Leebov, W. (1990), *Positive Co-worker Relationships in Health Care*, American Hospital Publisher, ASIN: B000MIM530.

Mayo Clinic, http://www.mayoclinic.com/health/stress/WL00049.

Sarkar, D. (2006), *5S for Service Organizations and Offices: A Lean Look at Improvement*, American Society for Quality, Milwaukee, WI.

Scholtes, P., *An Elaboration on Deming's Teachings on Performance Appraisal*, Joiner Associates, Madison, WI, 1987.

TribuneIndia.com (1999), Personal discipline: (http://www.tribuneindia.com/1999/99apr25/sunday/option.htm).

Tucker-Ladd, C. (2005), *Psychological Self-Help*, http://www.psychologicalselfhelp.org/.

Index